Ditching the Diapers Just Got Easier!

Welcome to Your Stress-Free, Tantrum-Free Guide to Potty Training

THE SIMPLEST Potty Training BOOK IN THE WORLD

Printed in China

First edition, AUG 2024

Paperback ISBN: 9781736894736

Library of Congress Control Number: 2024923902

To order additional copies of this book or for volume purchases and resale, send inquiries to: info@simplestbaby.com

Published by Simplest Company

Los Angeles, CA

simplestbaby.com

THE
SIMPLEST™
POTTY
TRAINING
BOOK IN THE WORLD

Ditch the Diapers!
The Stress-Free, Tantrum-Free
Guide to Potty Training

S.M. Gross

Jeremy F. Shapiro, MD, MPH, FAAP

Suzi Schwartz, Potty Training Expert

and the *Simplest Baby Community*

SIMPLEST COMPANY LLC.

DON'T PANIC, YOU GOT THIS

WHY YOU NEED THIS BOOK

For this book, we assume:

- You are not sure when to begin potty training.

- You are tired of changing dirty diapers.

- You want to start preparing for potty training.

- You feel it is time for your little one to be potty-trained.

- You are sick of spending money on diapers.

- You want your child to have greater independence.

- Your day care or school requires children to be potty-trained.

- You are looking for troubleshooting advice and tips.

- You want to avoid the horror stories you've heard.

- You are overwhelmed and need simple solutions.

- You want honest, no BS information on pottying.

NOTE: This book includes some advice for the various phases of training repeated throughout multiple sections. Just like practice makes perfect with potty training, repeated reading will allow parents to absorb the information more thoroughly at any and all stages of potty training their child.

WHAT'S IT ALL ABOUT?

Get ready to conquer the diaper days and make potty training a breeze. No nonsense, no fluff, just pure practical advice. We get it, you're not interested in decoding complicated parenting jargon. You want straightforward advice that works, and that's exactly what you'll find in this book. It's potty training for today's parents, designed to help you navigate through the messy terrain of potty training.

Our approach is simple: we take the best expert advice and distill it to the essentials. We've ditched the boring stuff and filled the pages with tips and tricks that are relatable to today's parents. From potty readiness signs to handling the inevitable oops moments, we've got you covered.

But we're not stopping there! We've sprinkled in some humor because, let's face it, potty training can be a comedy of errors. You'll laugh, you'll learn, and most important, you'll conquer the potty training challenge like a pro.

Ditch the diapers and embrace the potty revolution! With The Simplest Potty Training Book in the World, you'll be well-equipped to guide your toddler to diaper independence. Read this book now and say hello to a world of clean triumphs and fewer diaper blues!

MY STORY

As a new dad, I didn't know much about raising kids and didn't have a strong support group, living far from both our families. I found the information out there—books, websites, blogs, videos, etc.—all too dense, overwhelming, and not simple enough for today's needs.

I did a lot of research through countless conversations with a community of those who know best—moms, dads, nurses, doctors, nannies, educators, etc.—and distilled it down to the essentials.

I realized that if I had these challenges, other new parents must too.

And that is where the idea for the Simplest series came from—our desire to share this collective knowledge in a way that provides new parents with the solutions they need quickly and easily. We wanted to create a safe place that invited parents to share their experience and knowledge with each other.

CONTENTS

CHALLENGES & SOLUTIONS
Learn how to handle common potty training challenges, from fear of flushing to toileting anxiety, constipation, urinary tract infections, potty regression and setbacks, and much more.
PAGES: 115–148

OVERNIGHT TRAINING
What you need to know about the difference between daytime training vs. overnight training, strategies for dealing with bed-wetting, and other essential overnight training tips and advice.
PAGES: 149–156

TRAINING SCRIPTS
Practical tips, phrases, and ways to speak with your child to help them achieve potty training success and reduce the overall stress for both of you.
PAGES: 157–166

ADDITIONAL THOUGHTS
Closing thoughts and advice.
PAGES: 167–168

Understanding shit & getting your crap together

SIMPLEST METHOD

An overview of the Simplest method, how it works, and key things to know and do before you start training.

SIMPLEST™
POTTY TRAINING
METHOD

1. START BY UNDERSTANDING THE BIG PICTURE

Determine if your child is ready to begin potty training.

2. TRAINING PREPARATION

Understand what you need for potty training. Review the Simplest method, begin preparing for training, and determine if there are any specific adjustments needed for your child and family.

This book is intended to:

- Provide the key fundamentals for potty training.
- Distill all the potty training information down to its essentials.

Potty training is a big milestone and can be a bit daunting and overwhelming. We understand that today's parents are overworked and overscheduled, so we have created a resource that provides quick, to-the-point steps and scripts to help simplify the process.

AND GET FREE SIMPLEST™

QR Codes activate FREE content

Scan the QR codes throughout the book for quick access to **FREE** additional resources like must-haves, tips, organizing tools, charts, etc. that complement the book and make your potty training journey much easier.

TIPS & SHORTCUTS

Sprinkled throughout the book you will find these helpful tips.

 QUICK TIPS Small, practical recommendations that help make potty training easier.

 Mommy Hacks Parents' simple solutions and clever workarounds for training issues.

3. START TRAINING

Then follow the practical step-by-step outline on how to implement the Simplest Potty Training method.

PLUS

LEARN THE BASICS FOR DEALING WITH:

Accidents

Power Struggles

Regression

Health Concerns

Hygiene

Toileting anxiety

Scripts, and much more.

ESSENTIAL TOOLS!

Essential Lists

Product Recommendations

Illustrated Charts

THE SIMPLEST™ METHOD
WHAT'S IT ALL ABOUT

Ready to get started? Here's how potty training the Simplest way works:

METHOD OVERVIEW

The Simplest Potty Training method is a gradual, gentle, stress-free way to transition your little one from diapers to the potty! Our step-by-step program adapts to your child's unique pace, ensuring comfort and confidence at every stage.

The process is broken down into three simple and distinctive phases.

PREPARE ➤ **PRACTICE**

PREPARE PHASE
Outlines the various ways you can lay the foundation for the potty training process.

PRACTICE PHASE
The steps, scripts, and activities you'll need to actively potty train your child.

IT'S A PROCESS

Understanding potty training is a process—a process that requires:

- **REPETITION**

  Like everything else your child learns, showing your child how to do something once does not mean they will get it. You have to show them over and over again. Repetition is required.

- **PRACTICE**

  Like the saying goes, "Practice Makes Perfect." It is soooooo true for potty training. Like all learning, there will be mistakes and accidents. It is from those mistakes that we learn, so you should expect accidents.

- **BUILDING BLOCKS/PHASES**

  Like learning many new skills, it requires that we learn one part first so that we can build on it to learn the second part and so on. Potty training is like that too.

SUSTAIN PHASE

Once your child has successfully shown they know how to use the potty, this stage works at locking in those lessons and helps them with continued pottying success.

THE SIMPLEST METHOD™

DITCH THE STRESS

A gentle and gradual potty training method that combines the very best techniques and expert guidance.

IS IT RIGHT FOR YOU?

Not for you if:

- You are in a hurry.
- You lack the time or patience.
- You can't follow all the steps.

For you if:

- You are not in a rush.
- You want a more gentle approach.
- You want to avoid as much stress as possible on you and your child.
- You are interested in a gradual and natural approach.

Preparation

The idea is to take more time up front to lay the foundation for training.

KEY ASPECTS

One of the key differences between the Simplest Potty Training method and other methods is the time we take up front preparing for training.

Potty training should not be so stressful!

Through various activities in the preparation phase, the Simplest method takes a bit more time up front in order to gradually introduce the concept of pooping, peeing, and the pottying process. This process spans several months prior to beginning active training.

Why do we do this?

Introducing potty training in this gradual manner plants the seeds for potty training in a natural and easy way—so when your child is ready to actually potty train, it happens a bit more seamlessly and less stressfully. By the time you begin active training, the concept of pooping and going to the potty won't be new to your child, as it has already been part of your child's play and part of their world for some time.

This early preparation can make training easier and less fearful for your child, as they will already be familiar with peeing and pooping on the potty.

Timelines and schedules

There is no set schedule or timeline. Each step depends solely on your child's development, interest, and readiness. This method takes more time up front to lay the foundation for potty training so that when you reach each step in the process, it happens more seamlessly, with less stress and pressure on you and your child than other methods.

There is **NO** rush

This method takes its time and gently progresses at your child's pace, directed by you.

While your child determines the timing for moving to the various phases in the method, you will play an active role in helping to guide and direct the overall process.

SIGNS OF READINESS

ARE WE THERE YET?

Determining if your child is ready for potty training is less about their age and more about their emotional, mental, and physical readiness.

WHEN TO BEGIN

It's important to keep in mind that every child is different and develops at their own pace. Many children are ready to begin toilet/potty training between 18 and 30 months, but others may not be ready until they are three years old, and few, but some, may be ready before 18 months. Most children are trained by four years old.

Instead of focusing on the age of your child to determine when to begin potty training, parents should **focus on their child showing several of the signs of readiness** on the opposite page. The more signs, the better.

The sweet spot for potty training is around

20 to 25 MONTHS

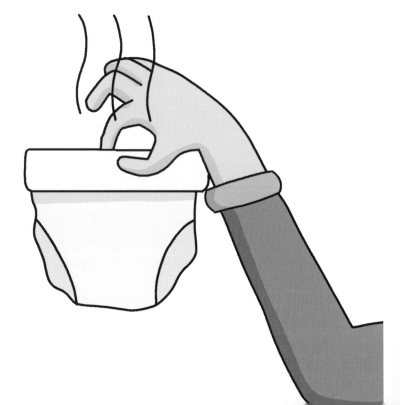

Mommy Hack
"Nanny Advice"
Around the 20 to 25 month period, check your child's diaper every hour and record how long between changes. If your child is dry from morning to midday, they may be ready to begin potty training.

SIGNS OF READINESS

COMMUNICATION

Your child is able to communicate either verbally or nonverbally.

UNDERSTANDS & FOLLOWS DIRECTIONS

Your child can follow the simple steps of going potty. These include pulling down pants, sitting on the potty, going, flushing, etc.

STAYING DRY

Your child staying dry for two or more hours is a sign they are developing bladder control and might be ready to begin potty training. Your child tends to be dry after naps.

TAKING PANTS ON AND OFF

Child can pull and push their pants up and down.

WALKING & STANDING

Your child can stand, walk, and run.

THINGS ARE MORE REGULAR

Your child is going more consistently at the same time each day.

KNOWS WHEN THEY HAVE GONE

Your child can recognize their need to go or has gone and tells you verbally or through their body language that they have.

DISLIKES DIRTY DIAPERS

Your child does not like to be in a dirty diaper and wants to be changed.

SHOWS INTEREST

Your child is curious about the toilet or actually wants to sit on it. They may also be interested in watching others go to the bathroom.

HIDES

Your child starts hiding when they need to poop.

ASSERTS INDEPENDENCE

Your child says things like, "I can do it myself," or, "Me do!"

PERSONALITY & TRAINING

WORKING WITH YOUR CHILD'S PERSONALITY

When it comes to potty training, your child's personality and temperament play a role.

OVERVIEW

No one knows your child better than you. Understanding your child's personality and working with it can go a long way. By the time you are ready to begin potty training, you will know your child's key personality traits.

Your child's personality may fit just one type or be a combination of several. Whatever the case, you will need to tailor your approach to your child.

LAID-BACK, PEOPLE PLEASER

These children are eager to please and interested in learning about the potty. They really want your praise. You should make your praise specific to an achievement, not a generic "Good boy," or, "Good girl." You will need to guide them and provide extra encouragement.

STRONG-WILLED

Has a mind of their own. You tell them one thing and they may do another. Patience is key. Get them involved in the process by giving them choices. Let them choose the big toilet or the potty chair, choose the rewards, put the sticker on the potty chart, or decide the ringtone for the alarm reminder to go to the potty.

FREE SPIRIT

These curious children may need you to make the pottying experience as interesting as possible. You may need to help them focus, as they can be easily distracted by other things. Patience and persistence are key.

SHY

These children may need a little extra time to get used to the potty before actually using it. You may have to gradually expose this child to each aspect of the training process. Be very encouraging and patient.

THINKER, PERFECTIONIST

Such children want to do things right and want to know and understand the rules around potty training. A little more explanation is helpful, but keep it short. These children can be afraid of change and need lots of information. They tend to be cautious.

HIGH ENERGY, ADVENTUROUS

Always on the move—may need help slowing down to use the potty. May need some activities on the potty to keep them focused and on task. Tend to love attention and like to be involved, so framing things in a way that provides a choice can help keep them engaged.

BOYS VS. GIRLS
TRAINING DIFFERENCES

Every child is different, and while training boys vs. girls is basically the same, there are a few differences to be aware of.

Mommy Hack
BOYS PEEING
To get your son to keep his pee in the toilet, encourage him to aim by putting a few Cheerios, or a similar cereal, in the toilet bowl, and have him try to hit them while peeing.

WHICH WAY TO WIPE

One of the biggest differences to keep in mind between girls and boys is how you teach them to clean themselves after going to the bathroom.

Girls should be taught to always

WIPE FROM FRONT TO BACK,

and never rewipe with dirty toilet paper or a dirty wet wipe.

This is important because it keeps girls from introducing bacteria into the urinary tract that can cause Urinary Tract Infections (UTIs). There is less concern about which way boys wipe, as their anatomy makes them less prone to developing UTIs.

SHOULD I STAND or SHOULD I SIT

We recommend you start potty training with your child sitting first. You might prefer that sitting remains the only way your child pees, but it is inevitable that boys will soon start peeing while standing, so teaching your son to do it right will save you from continually cleaning pee off the floor.

Don't be surprised if your daughter also tries peeing while standing. However, girls usually don't like it and end up preferring to sit.

Generally, it's not about being a boy or a girl—it's more about the individual personality of the child. However, there may be some different tendencies between boys and girls.

BOYS	GIRLS
• May not be ready for training until several months later than girls.	• May show interest in potty training sooner than boys.
• May be more impatient with training.	• May be more patient.
• May get bored with rewards more quickly.	• May stick with one reward throughout the training process.
• May have more accidents.	• May have fewer accidents.

ARE "YOU" READY?

GETTING YOUR SH*T TOGETHER

Potty training can be frustrating and exhausting, so we have put together some tips and advice for dealing with the potty training blues.

QUICK TIP
SLEEP?
Important to note: if a child is not getting adequate sleep, it's not reasonable to expect that they will be able to master potty training.

TIPS FOR DEALING WITH STRESS

Dealing with the stress of potty training requires patience, resilience, and a supportive approach. Here are some strategies that may help you manage your stress during this process:

STAY CALM
Try to remain calm and patient when accidents happen. Your child will pick up on your emotions, so staying composed can help reduce their anxiety and yours.

SET REALISTIC EXPECTATIONS
Potty training is a process and accidents are normal. Set realistic expectations for both yourself and your child, and be prepared for setbacks along the way.

EDUCATE YOURSELF
Learn about the signs of readiness for potty training and the various approaches to the process. Knowledge and understanding can help alleviate some of the uncertainty and stress.

THINK OF ACCIDENTS AS A POSITIVE
Reframe in your mind that your child having an accident is actually a good thing, as it is an opportunity for them to learn. This can help you stay calm and reduce your stress.

STOP COMPARING
Every child is different, so resist the urge to compare your potty training to others. It will only stress you out.

SEEK SUPPORT

Speaking to others that have gone through this already is a good way to know that you are not alone. (Note: listen but don't judge yourself based on others' experiences.)

TAKE CARE OF YOURSELF

Remember to prioritize self-care during this stressful time. Make time for activities that help you relax and recharge, whether it's exercise, meditation, or spending time with loved ones.

STAY FLEXIBLE

Be willing to adjust your approach to potty training based on your child's needs and progress. What works for one child may not work for another, so staying flexible and adaptable is key.

SEEK PROFESSIONAL HELP IF NEEDED

If you're feeling overwhelmed or unsure how to proceed, don't hesitate to seek help from a pediatrician, counselor, or child development specialist. They can offer guidance and support tailored to your specific situation.

DON'T RUSH IT

Make sure your child is ready for training and don't let what anyone else thinks about when you should begin potty training affect your decisions for your child.

TAKE BREAKS

If you or your child is experiencing a heightened sense of anxiety, it might be wise to consider taking a break from potty training. It's okay to pause and revisit the process when everyone is feeling more relaxed.

TRAINING NO-NO'S
WHAT NOT TO DO OR SAY

Saying the right things is important, but not saying or doing other things is also important.

QUICK TIP

If your child is going through any changes or experiencing stress, like a new school, new home, difficulty at home, or the arrival of a new baby, it's best to hold off on potty training.

THINGS TO AVOID DURING TRAINING

DON'T FORCE IT

It is critically important that your child be developmentally ready for potty training. As much as we might want to have it done and over with, if your child is not ready, they are not ready. You **CAN'T** rush it. However, it is worth keeping in mind that most potty training will not be all smooth sailing. It can be hard and challenging, so don't give up on the first signs of any pushback.

NO NEGATIVE LANGUAGE

Potty training at times can be a frustrating, stressful, and upsetting process, but losing your temper and saying harsh things or showing frustration will not help. In fact, it can cause negative effects.

NO PUNISHMENT

Accidents are part of potty training, and when they happen, it is important not to punish your child. Your negative reaction can create a negative association with toileting and can hinder progress, so remain calm and positive.

SIT, STAY

It is one thing to take your child to the potty to try to go, but you should **NEVER** make them sit on the potty until they go. This is essentially a form of punishment. Typically, at least two to three minutes for peeing, and three to five minutes for pooping is standard.

DON'T ASK

"Do you want to go to the potty?" Asking your child allows them to tell you, "No," which they, more than likely, will say. It gives them a false choice. What kid is going to stop playing and having fun to go to the bathroom? Very few, if any.

ONLY REWARD SUCCESS

If you use rewards, only reward your child for successfully using the potty. Even a little pee or poop in the potty is a success and deserves to be celebrated.

CHOOSE THE RIGHT TIME

Do not begin potty training during a time of stress or change, like moving to a new home, a marriage, a divorce, a vacation, a new baby, a new school, a death, etc.

Potty
training
is not a
race.

PREPARE

This phase is all about laying the foundation for potty training, getting your child ready for the active training phase.

THE MUST-HAVES
FOR POTTY TRAINING

GET THE RIGHT STUFF!
Scan the QR code to easily get our recommendations to start your potty training off on the right foot with all the essentials you will likely need.

1–2 POTTY TRAINING CHAIRS
One of the most important items is a simple, easy-to-use potty chair that has a comfortable seat. It should be sturdy with no rough edges. Look for a two-piece design so that the bowl can be removed and cleaned easily. Having grips on the base for stability is a plus. It should have a splash guard, especially if your child is a boy.

15–20 PAIRS OF BIG BOY OR GIRL UNDERWEAR
Look for underwear that is made of comfortable, high-quality, organic cotton. It should be breathable, not too tight, with a smooth waistband and a durability that will hold up after multiple washes.

FLUSHABLE WET WIPES
Use unscented, hypoallergenic, paraben-and-fragrance-free wipes. Be sure that the wipes are biodegradable!

2–4 CHILDREN'S POTTY TRAINING BOOKS
Look for books about how to use the potty that are written for toddlers and are playful and fun.

1 TOILET SEAT REDUCER
Look for one that is contoured for comfort, fits snuggly on the toilet seat for stability, and has a splash guard. Ideally, it should have a hook or handle to help with storage and carrying.

KIDS' SOAP
Look for soap that is paraben-, fragrance-, alcohol-, phthalate-, sulfates-, and formaldehyde-free. One that is hypoallergenic and gentle on the skin.

1–2 STEP STOOLS
Get one that is sturdy, durable, and easy to clean. It should have anti-slip material on the top for when your child steps up on it for their feet to be firmly planted on the step. It should also be light enough for a child to pick up and move.

1 TRAINING CHART
Determining what you want to include in your training chart will depend on how you plan on using rewards/charts. Ideally, the chart or stickers have characters or graphics that your child loves, which will make it more fun and enjoyable for them.

CLEANING SUPPLIES
What you choose should have NO phosphates, chlorine, ammonia, brighteners, parabens, phthalates, or artificial colors and fragrances. Nontoxic!

REWARDS
Our recommendation is that rewards be something small, for example, stickers, a sweet treat, or doing an activity with your child, etc.

1–2 MATTRESS PROTECTORS/COVERS
Look for an absorbent, comfortable, waterproof cover that is easy to clean and will hold up to frequent washing.

POTTYING PREP

PREPARATION OVERVIEW

"Proper preparation prevents poor performance."
Nowhere is this more evident than when potty training.

Mommy Hack

We don't recommend purchasing a specific character potty. However, if you do want your child to feel it is their potty, you can have them decorate it with removable character stickers.

NOTE: Every child is different, and starting dates will vary depending on your child's readiness and development. The **PREPARATION PHASE** of the Simplest method generally begins at around the 14 to 18 months mark.

LET'S TALK

Talk, talk, talk. You're going to be talking a lot about the potty throughout the preparation phase. Each activity of this phase consists of sharing and talking about pottying or narrating the process. The activities are intended to make learning about pottying fun—so when you talk about it, you should be upbeat and playful.

Well before you begin training, you should start talking about "feeling" the need to pee and poo, randomly adding it into your everyday conversations. See the spread "I Got a Feeling" on pages 31–32.

BUY A POTTY CHAIR

At around 18 months, we suggest you buy a potty chair. You don't have to involve your child in deciding which potty to purchase. We suggest buying a generic one, especially if you have or are planning to have additional children. This way you can use the potty chair for future training.

Place the potty in the bathroom with your child. Check out the spread on "Introduce the Potty," pages 35–36. We recommend a potty chair, and if your child insists on peeing or pooping just like Mommy or Daddy on the big toilet, we suggest you get a seat reducer for the toilet. (You will need one later when transitioning to the big toilet from the potty chair.)

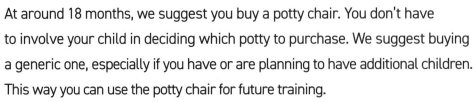

POO WITH YOU

Starting when your child is around 18 months, consider bringing her with you when you go to the bathroom, now and again.

Children are naturally curious, and typically, most will be very interested in what you are doing. Check out the "Pooing with You" spread on pages 41–42 for how to use going to the bathroom as an opportunity to help your child learn about using the potty.

POTTY VIDEOS

Start sprinkling some playful potty videos about going to and using the potty into your child's screen time. See our spread "Potty Books & Videos" on pages 43–44 for our recommendations.

POTTY BOOKS

Starting around 14 to 18 months, you can begin reading children's books about poop and using the potty. There are many great potty-themed books that are fun and entertaining. Sprinkle them in with the other books that you already read to your child during the day and at night. Do this for several months.

LET'S PLAY POTTY

Play is an amazing tool to help children learn. We recommend using it to help your child understand how to use the potty. We suggest using a stuffed animal or doll to show your child how to potty. See the spread on "Let's Play Potty" pages 37–38.

CHOOSE YOUR WORDS

Decide the words you will use to describe the various aspects of potty training. Keep potty words simple, and avoid words you don't want your child to use.

GET PREPARED

As you begin preparing your child for potty training, you should also begin getting everything you will need for training. Check out our list of potty-training must-haves.

Potty training can be stressful, and it is wise to begin reading various books, watching videos, etc. to ensure you too are personally prepared for potty training.

PREPARE THE BATHROOM

WHAT YOU NEED TO BEGIN

Before you start, make sure you have everything you need ready for potty training.

TOWELS
Make sure your child can reach the towels.

SEAT REDUCER
Either install a seat reducer or have a removable one in a place where your child can easily get to it.

POTTY CHAIR
Place the potty chair in the bathroom in a place that is easy for your child to access and use.

STOOL
Place a small stool next the toilet so that your child can mount the toilet and use it to place their feet on while going to the bathroom.

SOAP
Purchase and place child-appropriate soap where your child can easily reach it.

QUICK TIP
We recommend the potty chair only go in the bathroom, so you reinforce the idea that it is the correct place to go potty. Placing the potty chair anywhere else risks it becoming a toy box or covered in toys.

STEP STOOL
Have a sturdy stool for your child to use to wash their hands at the sink, so they can easily reach the faucet, soap, and towels.

CHOOSE YOUR WORDS

A FEW CHOICE WORDS

It's important when potty training to communicate in a way that is clear, positive, and encouraging to your child.

WHERE TO START

One of the things we suggest you do first is agree on what words you will use to describe the pottying process and your child's anatomy.

We recommend you keep potty words simple and avoid words you don't want your child to use. Once you have decided on the specific words you will use, be sure to share them with your partner, nanny, family, school, etc., so everyone involved in the potty training process knows the words to use.

JUST WORDS

It is important to understand that the words you are using are new to your child. The words themselves don't hold any positive or negative meaning. They are parts of the body—like finger, hand, or nose—and are part of the natural process of going to the bathroom.

Any other meaning is solely in our heads as parents. The words themselves do not have any sexual connotation, shame, or negative association to your child. They are just words.

Children are very sensitive to their parents and pick up on their subtle emotional cues, so when using the various words, be mindful not to let any personal feelings of discomfort or embarrassment come across. Stay positive and upbeat.

PROCESS WORDS

Decide on what words to use for your child's bodily fluids and bowel movements.

Bowel Movements:
- Poop
- Poo
- Number 2
- Doo-doo

Urination:
- Pee
- Wee
- Number 1
- Tinkle
- Urine

Location of Toilet:
- Bathroom
- Restroom
- Toilet
- Little boys' room
- Little girls' room

ANATOMICAL WORDS

Decide what words you're going to use for private parts of boys and girls.

Backside Anatomy:
- Butt
- Tush/tushy
- Anus
- Rear
- Bottom

Boys' Anatomy:
- Penis
- Willy

Girls' Anatomy:
- Vagina
- Vulva

QUICK TIP

We recommend using the actual anatomically correct words for your child's body parts, like: penis, vagina, vulva, anus, scrotum, and testicles.

GET THE MESSAGE

SIGNS YOUR CHILD NEEDS TO PEE & POOP

Understanding and recognizing the signs of your child needing to go to the bathroom are critical to successful potty training.

SIGNS OF NEEDING TO GO

Usually, each child has their own set of signs that they display when they need to go to the bathroom. However, there are some typical "Gotta Go" signals you should recognize.

YOUR CHILD TELLS YOU

You're more than halfway home if your child tells you they need to go.

FACIAL EXPRESSIONS

Your child might make strange faces, grit their teeth, look concerned, or have a blank stare.

FIDGETING/ WIGGLING

What some call the pee-pee dance is a telltale sign of needing to go.

CROSSING OR CLOSING LEGS

This can be a sign your child is trying to hold the pee.

HOPPING

Continually moving from one foot to another or one tiptoe to another.

AVOIDING EYE CONTACT

Some children will avoid looking you in the eye when they have to go, even when speaking with you.

GRUNTING

Your child is making strange noises while looking at or talking to you.

GRABBING PRIVATES

Holding or grabbing their privates is another way toddlers try to hold their pee and a sign of needing to go.

PASSING GAS

Passing gas is a common occurrence when needing to poop.

HIDING

Children might find an isolated spot, hiding behind furniture or drapes to poop or pee.

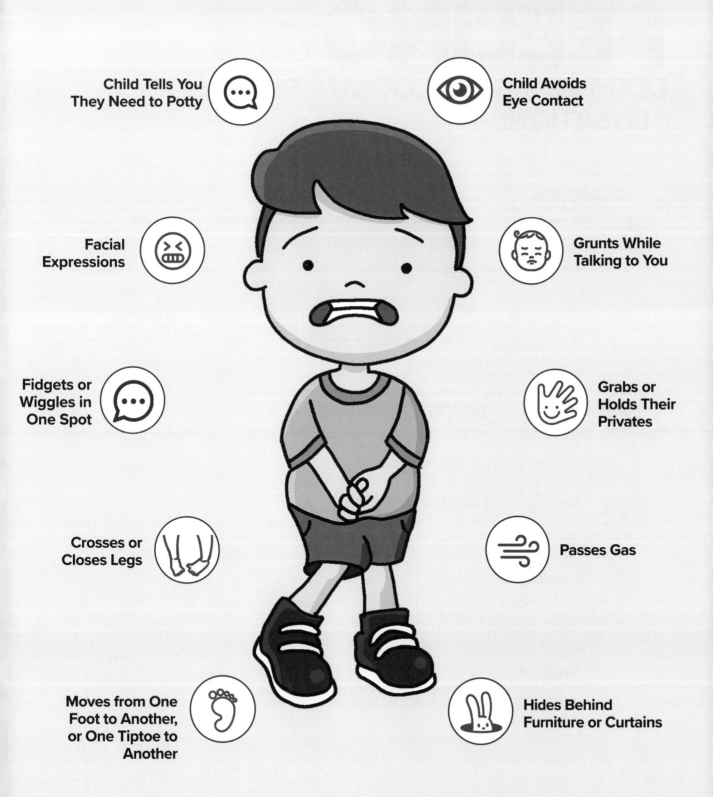

I GOT A FEELING
LEARNING TO RECOGNIZE BODILY SENSATIONS

OVERVIEW

A key component to the overall success of potty training is getting your child to recognize and connect the feelings of fullness or needing to pee or poop with actually going to the bathroom.

You can begin by helping to lay the foundation for recognizing and connecting a bodily urge or feeling to a specific physical activity by talking about similar feelings.

HOW TO DO IT—BEFORE TRAINING

One way to do this is to use the feelings their body experiences in other areas that are connected to a specific action, such as:

Connecting feelings of **hunger to eating.**

For example, in the morning, with a happy, upbeat tone of voice, you might say something like:

"Are you hungry? Do you want something to eat?"

"Yes."

"Oh good, your tummy must be telling you that it wants something yummy to eat?"

"What does your tummy feel like it wants to eat?"

Bend down to place you ear to your child's tummy, listening. Prompt your child to speak for their tummy. Then list the possible things your child likes, pausing to listen to their response.

Cereal? (pause) Pancakes? (pause) Eggs? (pause)

"Yes."

You might also use your own feelings of hunger to try and connect the feeling to having something to eat.

*"My tummy is growling and telling me it's hungry.
I need something to eat too."*

Connecting feelings of **thirsty with drinking.**

*"I would like something
to drink."*

"Are you feeling thirsty?"

"Yes."

*"OK, if your body is telling you
it needs something to drink,
then let's get something (water, milk, etc.)
for you and your body."*

WHERE DOES IT GO?

REINFORCE WHERE POO AND PEE GO

Around 14–18 months you should begin showing your child where poop and pee go.

WHERE POO & PEE GO

At this point your child is still wearing a diaper or pull-ups, and when they have a poopy diaper, take your child to the bathroom to change the dirty diaper/pull-up. Remove the diaper/pull-up, making sure your child can see you as you take the dirty diaper/pull-up to the toilet and shake the poop into it.

As you do, tell them:

"This is where poop and pee go."

Don't flush right away. Allow them to see the poop in the toilet. You can ask them if they want to flush the poo away. When flushing the toilet, in a fun, positive voice say,

"Bye-bye, poo-poo."

You should randomly repeat this process three to five times a week. You might change it up by asking while changing their diaper/pull-up:

"Where does poop and pee go?"

Wait for an answer, but if you don't get the correct one, you should happily tell them:

"Poop and pee go in the toilet."

THE POOP PROCESS

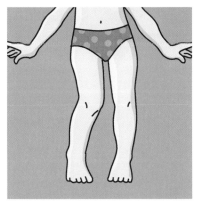

I POOPED

When your child has pooped in their diaper or pull-up, use it as a learning opportunity.

LET'S GO

Take your child and the dirty diaper/pull-up to the bathroom.

EMPTY IN TOILET

While your child watches, take the dirty diaper or pull-up and empty the poop in the toilet. At the same time, tell them that this is where poop goes.

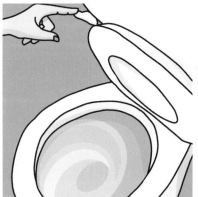

BYE-BYE POO-POO

Let your child see the poop in the toilet. Ask them if they would like to flush the poop down the toilet.

INTRODUCE THE POTTY

WELL, HELLO THERE

Getting a potty chair is an absolute must for potty training. Here is what you need to know and consider when buying one.

BUYING A POTTY

When your child is around 18 months of age, it's time to buy a potty chair. You don't have to involve your child in deciding which potty chair to purchase if you don't want to.

There are many different styles of potty chairs on the market—from the very simple to the very elaborate ones that make sounds, play music, look like characters, etc. We recommend that you choose one that is simple and a bit generic, especially if you have—or plan on having—another child you will need to train. This way you can use the potty for other children without a specific color, character, or theme becoming an issue.

With your child, place the potty in the bathroom, explaining to them that it's a special chair just for them.

"This is a special chair just for you. As you get bigger, you will use it to go pee and poo, just like Daddy and Mommy do."

Using simple and positive language, talk to your child about using the potty and explain what the potty is for and how it works. Encourage them to ask questions, and listen for any concerns they might have.

The goal is to make the potty as familiar and nonthreatening as possible. Let your child explore it and become comfortable with it.

LOOK FOR A POTTY CHAIR THAT:

- Has a removable bowl or basin.
- Is easy to empty.
- Is comfortable to sit on.
- Is sized for your child.
- Is stable and will not tip over.

- Has a nonslip base for safety.
- Is easy to clean.
- Has a splash guard for boys.
- Is lightweight.

A SEAT REDUCER

A seat reducer is a device that fits on top of a standard toilet seat. It reduces the size of the opening, so it fits a toddler more comfortably.

We recommend you begin training with a potty chair, however, you might also consider getting a seat reducer. Eventually your child will transition to the standard toilet, and we recommend a seat reducer when this occurs.

LOOK FOR A SEAT REDUCER THAT:

- Has a snug fit in the standard toilet seat.
- Has a nonslip liner to prevent slipping.
- Is lightweight.
- Is contoured to fit your toddler.

- Has a splash guard for boys.
- Has handles or grips.
- Is easy to clean.

DECORATING THE POTTY

To make the potty specific to your child, you can make decorating the potty a fun activity you do together. Purchase some of your child's favorite removable stickers and let your child place them on the outside of the potty.

Once your child has outgrown the potty, you can simply remove the stickers so you can use the same potty for your other children.

LET'S PLAY POTTY

EXAMPLE

Children often learn best through play. Role-playing with a stuffed animal is a fun way to teach your child how to use the potty.

QUICK TIP

You can use one of your child's favorite plush toys or dolls to help potty train your toddler. Just make sure the toy has long enough legs so that you can put real underwear and pants on it.

HOW IT WORKS

Before your child begins potty training, you can use a stuffed animal or doll to role-play the pottying process.

It's ideal to use a plush toy that you can actually put a real diaper or pull-ups and pants on. This way you can simulate the full experience of going to the potty. This experience should be fun and upbeat. Remember: this is play.

Mommy Hack

If your child has picked out their favorite underwear for the practice phase of training, you might consider using them for Teddy to wear during potty play. That is if your child will let Teddy wear them.

PLAY POTTY SCRIPTS

"I think Teddy needs to go potty."

"Teddy, do you need to try and go potty?"

Act as if Teddy said that he does need to go to the potty.

"OK, Teddy, let's go. Come on, (child's name), let's take Teddy to the potty."

Tell your child:

"(Child's name), we are going to have to help Teddy and show him what to do. He has never gone to the potty before."

Go with your child and Teddy to where the potty is. On the way, tell Teddy:

"Teddy, I'm so proud of you. This is so exciting, and it's great that you are going to use the potty."

Once at the potty, ask your child:

"What do you think Teddy should do first? "

Listen to the suggestions. If you don't get the right answer you want, suggest other answers.

"I wonder, maybe Teddy should take his pants and diaper off first so he doesn't get pee or poo on him. What do you think?"

"Can you help me take down Teddy's pants and diaper?"

Working together, take Teddy's pants and diaper/pull-up down. Then sit Teddy on the potty, telling Teddy:

"Take your time, Teddy. Try and go pee or poop. (Your child's name), in the meantime, should we read a story or play a game with Teddy?"

LET'S PLAY POTTY
EXAMPLE—CONTINUED

Children learn best through play, and role-playing with a stuffed animal is a fun way to teach your child how to use the potty.

QUICK TIP

Don't hesitate to get creative and add in scenarios that match your child's own situation. Every child is different and will have their own needs. Always be upbeat, playful, and positive. Other scenarios:
- Teddy washes his paws.
- Teddy missed the potty.
- Teddy had an accident.

Every now and again, ask your child to check if Teddy went.

"(Child's name), did Teddy go pee or poo yet?"

Your child can check and will tell you yes or no. If yes, you can proceed to the next step.

"Teddy—amazing—you did it! This is so exciting.
Teddy, you did a great job. (Child's name), and I are
soooo proud of you! Are you finished, or are
you still going more?"

When Teddy is finished, you can move to the next step.
If Teddy pooped (the same applies for peeing), you can say:

"Now that Teddy is done going poop, I think it is time to clean Teddy's bottom."

Ask your child:

"(Child's name), what do we do first?
Yes, we need some toilet paper to wipe
Teddy's bottom clean."

Show your child how much toilet paper to take and how to fold it, and then show your child the proper way to wipe Teddy's bottom.

"Oh, I did not get Teddy completely clean. He still has poo-poo on his bottom. Can you help me wipe Teddy? I will hold Teddy, and you can wipe him."

When clean, say:

"Now we can put Teddy's diaper/pull-up and pants back on."

Have your child help you get Teddy's clothes back on.

"Teddy, I'm so impressed—you pooped in the potty. You are becoming such a big bear now."

"(Child's name), now that Teddy is done, what do we do next?"

Listen to your child's answer. If, after a bit, you don't get an answer, you can say:

"I think we need to put the pee or poop where it belongs. Where do you think that is? Yes—the toilet."

Pick up the potty bowl and shake it into the toilet just as you would if it were real. Ask,

"Do you want to flush the poop or pee away?"

After repeating the role-play several times, Teddy can graduate to big bear underwear.

"(Child's name), wow, Teddy is doing such a good job. He has not wet his diaper and has been going to the potty so well. What do you think, is Teddy ready for big bear underwear?"

"(Child's name), do you want to put Teddy's new underwear on him? I can help you."

POOING WITH YOU
EXAMPLE

GOING WITH YOU

I know this can be a bit weird for some parents, but remember, peeing and pooping are natural bodily functions—everyone does them. They are not strange, gross, or bad.

Somewhere around 14 to 18 months, depending on your child, when you need to pee or poop, start taking your little one with you every now and then. You might say:

"Oh, I feel like I need to go pee or poop—I'm going to go to the bathroom now. Let's go to the potty together."

"How about you sit with me while I go potty? You can see how it's done."

Your child can either sit on their potty or stand, watching what you do.

NARRATE/SHOW EVERYTHING

It might feel odd, but you will need to explain everything you do. Use an upbeat and playful tone of voice. Yes, you will let them see everything, so they can model what you do when they try to use the potty themselves.

PEEING

- "I lift the toilet lid."
- "I pull down my pants and underwear."
- "I sit on the toilet/potty."
- (Boys) "I aim/push my penis down in the potty/toilet."
- "And I pee."

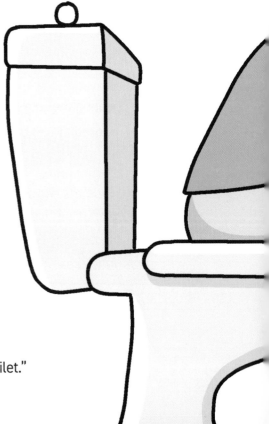

Let your toddler see the pee going into the toilet. Dads, if you are not comfortable being totally exposed, you can somewhat hold your penis down while peeing, which will also cover most of the top of your privates with your palm.

- (For boys) "I shake off the rest."
- (For girls) You will want to show her how to pat rather than rub her vagina dry.
- "Next, I pull up my underwear and pants."
- "I then flush the pee away." You can flush the toilet or let your child do it.

POOPING PROCESS

- "I lift the toilet lid."
- "I pull down my pants and underwear."
- "I sit on the toilet."
- "I relax and let the poop go. If it does not want to go, I use my muscles to give a little push."
- "If it still does not want to come, I stop and try again later."
- "If it comes, I let it go and wait to see if there is more."
- "When I think I'm done, or there is no more, I wipe my bottom." (See the spread on pages 83–84.)

Most children are curious to see what you have done, so don't be surprised if your toddler wants to look in the toilet. Let them. Show them the proper way to wipe themselves until they are clean.

- "I then pull up my underwear and pants."
- "I then flush the poop away." You can flush or let your child do it.

"Bye-bye, poo-poo."

AWKWARD QUESTIONS

What if they ask me about my privates?

Children are curious and want to understand everything, so don't be surprised or panic. Be prepared.

Your goal is to encourage appropriate behavior without creating any feelings of shame.

POTTY BOOKS & VIDEOS
WELCOME TO STORYTIME

One great way to help prepare your child is with stories and videos about potty training.

OVERVIEW

Stories can be a wonderful way to introduce your child to and help them learn about the potty and how it works. The stories are not only fun but educational.

BOOKS

There are many children's picture books about potty training on the market. We find it helps if you sprinkle these books in with the other storybooks you and your child read during the day or with the books you read before bed.

This is a great way to introduce the topic in a safe and playful manner so that when it is time to actually potty train, your child is familiar with the process. They will gain an understanding about what is expected of them.

You can use these books during potty training, including them among the books you read to your child while they are on the potty.

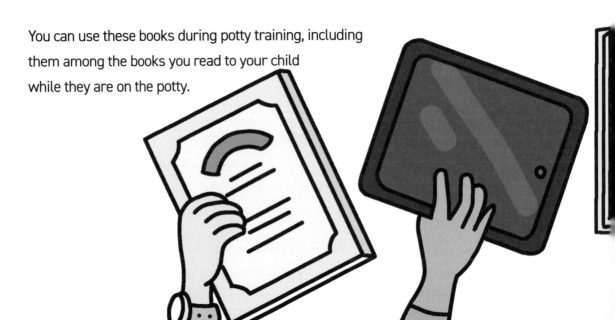

VIDEOS

The internet is full of lots of great content to help introduce your child to the potty. From silly stories to fun songs covering everything from peeing and pooping to wiping and washing their hands.

NOTE: We suggest you don't use the videos while your child is on the potty, as they can distract them from getting down to business (if you know what I mean). Your child might just want to go on watching videos rather than peeing or pooping. The videos are best used as a tool to introduce the concept of pottying before actual training begins.

OUR FREE RECOMMENDATIONS

Scan the QR code to easily get our recommendations for some awesome children's books and videos about the potty and teaching your child how it works.

HAVE A SEAT
GETTING COMFORTABLE

One of the first steps in potty training is making sure your child is comfortable with the potty.

SITTING ON THE POTTY—CLOTHING ON

After laying the groundwork for potty training, your next step will be to encourage your child to sit on the potty chair fully clothed or wearing their diaper/pull-up.

While your child sits on the potty, you can sit on the floor in front of them. This should be a relaxed and enjoyable experience. You can keep them busy by doing something fun like reading a book, singing songs, or telling stories.

The whole intention of this is to ensure that your child is comfortable with the potty. Don't force them to sit. If they want to leave, that is completely okay, but gently encourage them to stay.

TIMING

This step might go by pretty easily, because you already have had the potty in the bathroom and have already been talking about the potty and doing other things. At this point, your child may already have tried sitting on the potty chair themselves. If so, great!

If your child has no issues with sitting on the potty with their clothing on, you can move onto the next step—sitting on the potty bare bottom.

SITTING ON THE POTTY—BARE BOTTOM

During this step, you encourage your child to sit on the potty bare bottom.

While your child is bare bottom on the potty, you can either sit on the floor like before (when they where sitting with clothing on) or you can sit bare bottom on the toilet to show them how it is done. Just like with clothing on, in order to keep them busy and seated on the potty, you can sing songs, tell stories, etc.

Don't expect your toddler to actually go pee or poop. If your child does pee, GREAT. If they don't, GREAT. This is still about getting them used to the sensation of sitting on the potty and getting into a comfortable routine.

For some children, bringing their plush teddy bear or doll with them and letting the child explain to them what they are doing—basically showing them how it is done—is a good way to reinforce the potty process and behavior.

NOTE: During this time, you will also want to begin having your child practice washing their hands after sitting on the potty and after every attempt to pee or poop.

Mommy Hack

To encourage your child to wash their hands, it can be helpful if your liquid soap is packaged with your child's favorite character on it or the bar of soap has a character on or inside it.

Soap

PICKING UNDERWEAR
LET'S GET SOME BIG KID UNDERWEAR!

There aren't many fun parts to potty training, however, picking your toddler's first pairs of underwear is one of them.

OVERVIEW

After wearing diapers for more than a year, transitioning to underwear can be a big step for your little one. To help that transition go more smoothly, we recommend beginning to talk about wearing underwear in conversations with your child.

"You are becoming such a big boy/girl. Soon you won't need to wear diapers. We will need to look at getting you some (big boy or girl) underwear just like Mommy's and Daddy's."

It can be helpful if your child knows other kids just a bit older than themselves that are already potty-trained and wearing underwear. You can then use them as an example too.

"Soon you are going to be wearing underwear just like your (friend, cousin, etc.), _____."

You may then want to either sit down with your child to look for underwear online or bring your child to the store to go shopping for underwear. You should try and make this as fun and exciting an activity as possible.

"(Child's name), let's go shopping for some fun underwear. What color do you think you would like?"

"Blue."

*"Wow, that's my favorite too!
What character would you like on your underwear?"*

"I don't know."

"What about dinosaurs . . . or trucks?"

"Dinosaurs, yes!"

With your child's help, you found the underwear they like. Now you should explain that once they start potty training they will get to wear this really amazing underwear.

WHAT TO LOOK FOR

Material

Soft and breathable materials like organic cotton or bamboo, for comfort.

Correct Fit & Size

Getting the right size and fit are important. You want underwear that is not too tight or too loose.

Tagless

Ideally, the underwear should not have a sewn-in label. Rather, look for ones that are tagless.

Durable

The underwear is going to experience a lot of washing, so it's important to buy underwear that is up to the challenge.

Style, Color, and Print

Choosing the graphics that are on the underwear is the fun part that kids love to participate in. Find the character or theme that your child loves and is very excited to start wearing.

OUR FREE RECOMMENDATIONS

Scan the QR code to easily get our recommendations for some awesome big boy or girl underwear.

ACCIDENT PROOFING
PREPARING YOUR HOME

The practice phase of potty training is a messy process, so it's wise to do some home prep before you get started.

WHAT TO CONSIDER

Before you get started, there are a few things to do and consider.

WHERE?

Decide where you are going to be doing the potty training.
We suggest that you do it in a room with hardwood or tile floors to help prevent rugs and carpeted areas from being soiled.

Once you have decided where you will be training, you will need to determine what things you might want to protect and how.

TIPS FOR POO-PARING YOUR HOME

COVER IT UP

If you are concerned about your furniture being peed or pooped on, you might want to protect it. You can cover furniture with towels, blankets, plastic trash bags, plastic painter drop cloths, or furniture slipcovers to prevent pee leaking into the cushions.

Some parents use puppy pee pads alone or covered with towels that their child can sit on.

ROLL 'EM UP

You might want to consider rolling up and putting away area rugs during potty training to protect them.

LIMIT THE AREA

Shut doors or block off areas of your home in order to contain where in your home the accidents may occur.

CARPETS

If you are trying to protect a carpeted area, you can put down a vinyl tablecloth. If this doesn't work for you, then consider changing the area that you will be hanging out in.

BE POO-PARED

It's best to have all the supplies you will be using for cleaning up handy so that you have them as soon as you need them—towels, paper towels, cleaning products, etc.

SQUATTING POSITION | **WHAT TO KNOW**

2 Lean forward slightly, resting your elbows on your knees.

1 Sit with your knees higher than your hips.

3 Straighten your spine.

4 Place your feet apart and flat on the stool or floor.

Same posture when using a potty chair.

5 Relax.

PROPER POTTY POSITION

The human body is made to squat when pooping. It is in this position that the muscles of the rectum area are able to relax more, allowing for easier pooping. This position also works with gravity to help pass the poop. This can be especially helpful for children who are experiencing constipation.

IT'S A DATE
CHOOSING WHEN TO BEGIN

Your child has shown several signs of readiness, has been moving through the preparation really well, and you feel they are ready. What should you do next?

PICK THE TIME

The next step is to decide when you want to begin the "practice phase" of training, which we also refer to as active potty training.

We suggest you choose a long weekend when you can dedicate a minimum of three solid days to potty training. A week would be even better, if you can swing it. For the three-day method, choose a long weekend where you will have no interruptions and you don't plan to do anything other than focus on your child and potty training.

PLAN THE DAYS

You will be spending the initial three to five training days at home, so you are going to need to plan ahead for some fun activities. It helps to have art projects, games, or other fun children's activities. **NO** digital, electronic games, videos, movies, or TV.

LOCATION

Decide where you want to begin potty training. We suggest that you begin active training (the practice phase) by limiting the rooms that you will utilize during the first three to five days. This will help contain the mess caused by accidents and, depending on the location, may be close enough to allow your child to get to the bathroom in time.

Mommy Hack

PLAN MEALS

Cook meals ahead of the three days you will be potty training so that you can stay 100% focused on your child and not on making meals for the family.

Let's get
this potty
started.

PRACTICE

This is the active phase of potty training, which outlines step-by-step what to do.

HAVE THE TALK

PREPARING YOUR CHILD

Several weeks ahead of beginning potty training, we suggest you have "The Talk" with your child. This is a simple chat about what will be happening during this phase of the potty training process.

THE TALK

Potty training is a big step and a huge change for your child.

Several weeks before you begin potty training, you will want to take a moment to walk your child through what is going to happen, how long it will take, and why it's important.

Some of this will be redundant, but that's okay—repetition is your friend. In simple and positive language, share with your child how they will be using the potty chair, what the potty is for, and how it works. Encourage them to ask any questions and listen for any concerns they might have so you can address them before you start.

All children like to know what to expect. It is important to explain in simple terms everything that will be happening during this upcoming practice phase of training.

Tell them that they are becoming a "big kid" and that they will be using the potty like you use the toilet. Let them know it's nearly time to say goodbye to those diapers/pull-ups—as they will not need them anymore.

We recommend that you lose the pull-ups during the day, and depending on your child and their age, potentially use them only for naps and overnight.

MORE TO SHARE

 Reinforce that they will be using their special potty chair just like Mommy and Daddy use the big toilet.

 Talk about how exciting it will be for them to get to wear their big boy or girl underwear that you both picked out.

Work on building up the day you will begin potty training so your child starts to look forward to it.

HOW IT WORKS

Explain to your child that on the first day they get to run around the house with no pants while they learn to pee and poop in the potty—how fun! Explain that you will be spending the day with them playing games, etc., together and helping them.

Once they reach the point of being able to tell you when they need to pee and poo, they will get to wear their NEW super cool underwear—so exciting!

If you will be using a potty chart and rewards, explain to your toddler that when they pee on the potty they get a sticker to place on their potty chart and get one treat (if you are using treats). When they poop on the potty, they get two stickers to put on their chart and two treats (if using treats).

Emphasize that when they feel the need to pee or poop, they should let you know so that, together, you can go to the potty.

WATCH YOUR MOUTH

BE MINDFUL OF WHAT YOU SAY

During training, knowing what NOT to say is just as important as knowing what to say. Here are some things you should know before getting started.

WHAT TO SAY?

It's important to keep the potty training experience positive and calm for your child. Be sure to use words and a tone of voice that are positive, encouraging, and upbeat.

WHAT <u>NOT</u> TO SAY?

Avoid negative words, such as dirty, yucky, or stinky when describing things. Do NOT use words that shame or make your child feel bad or discouraged.

Avoid saying things like:

> *"It's okay."*   or,   *"I am soooo frustrated."*

When an accident happens, you don't want your child to think that it is okay to pee or poop on the floor. It's not. You also don't want to shame them for having an accident.

Instead, say things like:

> *"Oops, I see you had an accident.*
> *Let's try to get the pee or poop in the potty next time."*

> *"We need to listen to our body—and when you feel you*
> *have to pee or poop, we go to the potty."*

Avoid saying things like:

"Don't worry, I'll clean it up."

Your child should be an active participant in their potty training, and having them help clean up their pee accident (it is best that you handle cleaning up the poop) will help connect in their mind what happens when they don't get the pee or poop in the potty.

Instead, say things like:

"I'll get some towels, and we can clean it up together."

Avoid asking and expecting them to go.

"Do you want to go to the potty?"

"Do you have to go potty?"

More than likely the answer will be **NO**. Generally, parents need to take the lead when it comes to going to the bathroom because, for a toddler, just about everything will be more interesting than going potty.

Instead, say things like:

"It's time to try and go potty."

"Let's go to the potty so you can get back to _____."

"It's time for our potty break."

while gently walking your toddler to the potty.

I GOT A FEELING

RECOGNIZING BODILY SENSATIONS

One of the keys to successful potty training is getting your child to recognize and connect the sensation of needing to go pee or poop with actually going to the bathroom.

OVERVIEW

Talking about the sensations of needing to pee or poop before actual training begins will help your toddler make that connection during training.

THE **GOAL**

Your child **connecting the feelings** of needing to pee or poop **with the action** of going to and using the potty.

TIPS FOR RECOGNIZING THE SENSATIONS

READ THE SIGNS

Your child may not have the words yet to communicate their need to go, so you'll need to be on the lookout for any signs that they need to go.

When you see the sign, take them to the potty, and explain that the sensations they are feeling mean they need to pee or poop, and they should go to the potty.

CATCH THEM IN THE ACT

Catching your child mid-pee or poop can be a teachable moment. You should pick your child up and take them directly to the bathroom whether they are just starting or finishing peeing or pooping.

While taking them to the bathroom, talk to them about the feeling they had of needing to pee or poop. The point is to help them become aware of those feelings and what to do when they have them.

Mommy Hack

Your child will either pee or poop while bare bottom. It is wise to have a couple towels within arm's reach so that when you see them going, you can catch them up in the towel to take them to the potty.

USE YOUR WORDS CONSISTENTLY

Being consistent with the words used to describe peeing and pooping will help streamline your communications, making it easier for your child to tell you when they recognize the need to go.

ROLE-PLAY

A great way to help connect the sensation with going to the potty is by literally showing your child when you personally have to go. You might say:

"I feel a tingle. I think I have to pee."

"I feel fullness. I think I need to poop."

"Oh, I'm feeling full and pressure"
(while touching your abdomen).
"I need to go pee-pee or poop. I'm going to go to the bathroom. Let's go together."

"Oh! I think I need to go potty. I have the feeling like I need to go."

before you go to the bathroom. You are using the words to help make the connection to the physical sensations and going to the potty.

CREATE A SCHEDULE
GET WITH THE PROGRAM

QUICK TIP
POTTY BREAK
It can be helpful to use a timer either on your phone or some other device to remind you and your child that it is time to take a potty break.

Establishing a pottying schedule and being consistent in its application is an important part to achieving potty training success.

OVERVIEW:

Throughout potty training, you will be utilizing a schedule to outline the times you will be taking your child to the bathroom to try and pee or poop. Maintaining a schedule is especially important in the first weeks of training, where establishing and sticking to a routine is essential.

YOU WILL BE TAKING POTTY BREAKS:

1. When your child shows any sign of needing to pee or poop.

2. At the set times you determined in your schedule.

WHAT A SCHEDULE CONTAINS

In creating your potty-break schedule, it will incorporate several times.

1. SET TIMES

Your schedule should incorporate some set times to take your child to use the bathroom. For example:

Morning: First thing after getting out of bed in the morning.

Meals: After every meal—breakfast, lunch, and dinner.

Naps: Before going down for a nap and after getting up from one.

Night: Just before going to bed at night.

Out & About: Any time before leaving the house.

2. YOUR SCHEDULED TIMES

This is the amount of time between each pottying attempt before taking your child to the bathroom for another potty break. We have outlined our recommendations for these scheduled times for pottying breaks. You can follow ours or modify the times to fit you and your child's specific needs.

OUR RECOMMENDED SCHEDULED TIMES

SCHEDULE TIMES / DURING THE FIRST THREE DAYS

During the first three days of active potty training, you will take your child to the potty every 20 to 30 minutes or any time your child shows a sign of needing to go. Your child probably won't need to go every time you take them, and that is perfectly fine. The point of doing this is to give your child frequent opportunities to successfully pee or poop in the potty.

SCHEDULE TIMES / AFTER 4–5 DAYS

After the initial three days (depending on your child's grasp of the pottying process, i.e., peeing or pooping in the potty), you can begin to progressively extend the time between potty breaks. You can move from 30 minutes to an hour, and from an hour to two hours, and so on—as long as your child continues to make progress.

ACCIDENTS

If you start to notice more frequent accidents occurring after extending the times between potty breaks, go back to the shorter potty break time schedule.

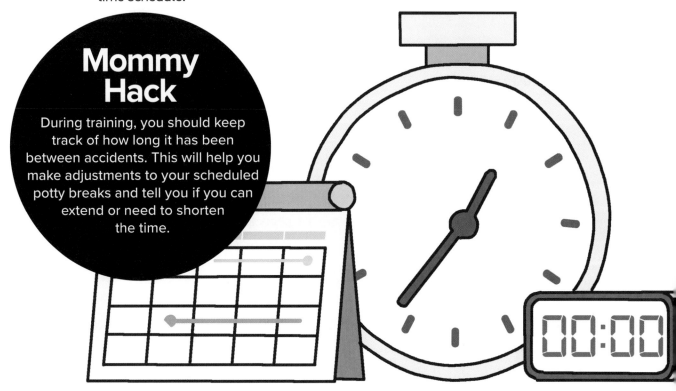

Mommy Hack

During training, you should keep track of how long it has been between accidents. This will help you make adjustments to your scheduled potty breaks and tell you if you can extend or need to shorten the time.

DAY 1
LET'S GET STARTED

You have prepared, set the stage, and picked the days to start active potty training. Here is a step-by-step guide for what you need to know and do during those first days.

Mommy Hack

WARM THINGS UP
Make sure the temperature in your house is warm enough so that when your child is bare bottom they don't get cold or try to cover themselves with a blanket.

The initial days of training are very important, as they establish a foundation for using the potty that you will build on and lock in over the subsequent weeks.

THE NIGHT BEFORE

The night before training, remind your child that tomorrow is the big day—when you will be saying bye-bye to diapers/pull-ups. You might say:

"Tomorrow is a big day. We say bye-bye to pull-ups and/or diapers. It's soooooo exciting!"

You have already walked your child through what will be happening, so they may be familiar with and understand what to expect. If you feel your child needs a refresher, go ahead and talk about it again.

GOOD MORNING

The day has arrived. When your child wakes up, tell them:

"Today is the big day. You no longer need to wear diapers because you will be peeing and pooping in the potty like we talked about."

We recommend that you let your child spend at least the first day, potentially even the second, bare bottom. Not wearing a diaper, underwear, or pants, your child is more likely to notice when they need to go to the potty. It will also help you see the signs that your child needs to go pee or poop, hopefully minimizing the number of messy accidents. Remember to have your child eat a good breakfast, drinking lots of liquids.

BYE-BYE DAYTIME DIAPERS

Then, together with your child, collect all the diapers to get rid of them for daytime use. You can make it a kind of a game, going around your home with a trash bag or box, placing all the diapers in it, and saying:

"It's time to collect all the pull-ups/diapers because you don't need to wear them anymore."

Whether your child helps or not, it's important for them to see you pretending to get rid of all the diapers. It helps if someone actually takes the diapers away while telling your child that:

"(Person's name) is taking the diapers to give to babies that need them."

The person can put them somewhere for safekeeping, but you want your child to believe that the diapers are gone for good (at least during the day).

LAST DIAPER

After collecting all the diapers, take your child to the bathroom and remove their diaper, leaving them bare bottomed. If they are wearing a shirt, make sure it is not too long and does not cover their privates. That way you can see if they start to go pee or poop. This is a good time to encourage them to try and go potty.

EXPLAIN AGAIN

Once again, reinforce what is happening today.

"Today is a very special day. I'm so proud of you for being such a big (girl or boy) today. When you need to go pee or poop, it's important that you let me know so we can go together."

While in the bathroom, explain how the potty chart works. You may be using a potty chart you found online or you can download our FREE Simplest potty chart. Whichever you choose, explain how it will work.

DAY 1
STEP-BY-STEP/CONTINUED

QUICK TIP

We recommend **NO** TV or iPad during active training. Kids become mesmerized by digital devices and will not be able to pull themselves away to go potty or communicate effectively.

POTTY BREAKS

You will be taking your child to the potty to try and pee and poop throughout the day based on the schedule you created. If they happen to go—GREAT—if not, that is FINE too.

Although they more than likely will not pee or poop the first time, you are beginning to establish a routine for going to the potty.

DRINK UP

During the morning and throughout the day, your child should drink plenty of liquids—water, juice, milk—whatever is their favorite. Natural fruit popsicles are another good way to have your child get some liquids too.

This will create the need for them to pee and opportunities for training. You want to give your child more fluids than normal but not so much that your child is peeing every five minutes.

It can also be helpful to offer salty snacks to your child to encourage them to drink more fluids.

KEEP AN EYE ON THEM

100 percent of your focus should be on your child, and they should not leave your sight. This is when being a helicopter parent can pay off. If you notice any signs that your child needs to pee or poop, quickly take them to the potty, saying:

"Remember, we pee and poop in the potty."

Some parents find it helpful to set a timer so that every 20 to 30 minutes it reminds not only you but your child that it's time to try and go potty again. This is especially helpful after meals or after having something to drink.

ACCIDENTS WILL HAPPEN

When accidents happen—and they will—don't get upset. Stay calm. Take note of about how long it took from the last time your child peed and any signals your child might have shown right before they had the accident. That way, next time, you may be able to catch them before the accident occurs.

NOTE: Do NOT ask your child if they have to go potty, expecting them to tell you. Instead, when it is time to go potty, say:

"Come on, it's time to try and go potty."

If you see any sign of an accident beginning to happen, pick up your child—even if it is mid-pee—and carry them to the potty, saying:

"Oh no, pee goes in the potty. Not on the floor."

Your child may stop peeing as soon as you pick them up. If so, they may not be completely finished. Make your way to the potty in a calm, unfrenzied way and place your child on the potty. Praise them for sitting on the potty:

"Wow, look at you, you're such a big boy/girl. Thank you for sitting on the potty so well."

If they happen to go even a little, give them lots and lots of praise.

"Hooray! You did it. Wow! You pee in the potty. This is fantastic! I am soooooooo proud of you. You did it, and I knew you could."

DAY 1
STEP-BY-STEP/CONTINUED

STAY POSITIVE

After the accident and they are finished in the bathroom, stay upbeat and positive. Then show them the pee on the floor, telling them:

"Your pee is on the floor. Pee and poop don't go here. They go in the potty. Next time, let's get the pee/poop in the potty."

FIVE-MINUTE WARNING

If after an accident your child does not pee or poop when taken to the potty, after about five minutes take them back to try again. Sit with them for a while. You can sing songs, tell stories, or just talk to keep them busy and help them stay seated.

After another five minutes, if nothing happens, praise them for sitting on the potty, and go back to what you were doing before the accident.

THEY PEED IN THE TOILET

If your child succeeded in peeing or pooping in the potty, it's time to celebrate. Give your child lots and lots of praise and big hugs and kisses.

Let your child know how proud you are of them. Do a little dance—whatever to express how amazing it is and how happy you are. If you are using a potty chart, it's time to mark it in the appropriate manner.

WASH UP

After every attempt, whether successful or not, you should show your child the proper way to wipe themselves and wash their hands.

COMMUNICATE

Throughout the process you should use language and a tone of voice that is positive and encouraging, whether they are successful at going or not, and even if they have an accident. No harsh words or displays of frustration and absolutely **NO** punishment if there is an accident.

Praise your child or use some reward every time they use the potty successfully (peeing or pooping in the potty).

Your praise is important, as it reinforces:
1) The desired behavior.
2) That your child actually peed or pooped in the potty correctly.

PROMPTS AND REMINDERS

Although you are going to be following your personal schedule for taking potty breaks, we recommend you still ask your child if they need to go potty. Will they let you know? **NO**—at least not yet—but keep asking. Repeat, repeat, repeat.

The reason for asking this way is to plant the seeds to get them to the point where they will take themselves to the potty and to also help them recognize that, yes, they have the feeling of needing to go potty. For example, 5–10 minutes before your scheduled potty break, you might ask:

"(Child's name), do you need to go potty?"

"No."

"OK, but in five minutes it will be time for us to go try to pee or poop."

DAY 1
STEP-BY-STEP/CONTINUED

PROMPTS AND REMINDERS CONTINUED

It is important to understand that children tend to get so distracted by just about everything and anything they are doing. The last thing they will want to do is stop playing and go potty. You need to be persistent.

If your child is in the middle of an activity when it's time for a potty break, don't abruptly take your child away from their activity. Instead, either allow your child to finish what they are doing (if brief) or tell them that in a couple minutes you are going to try and go potty. That way you minimize the potential of creating any negative association with going to the potty.

When it is time to try and go, you might say:

"It's *potty time.*" "*It's time to try and go potty.*"

"*It's time for a potty break.*" "*Potty break time.*"

"We listen to our body. When our body tells us we need to go, we go to the potty."

NARRATE THE PROCESS

During the various trips to use the potty, you should every now and again narrate the process. This will help your child learn the pottying process and steps. You can narrate the steps while they do the actions themselves.

For example:

POTTYING STEPS

1. *We take our pants and underwear down (when they have underwear or pants on—this may be more of a day three thing).*
2. *We sit on the potty and let the pee or poop go.*
3. *If the poop or pee doesn't come right away, we wait to let it come.*
4. *Once we have gone, we wait to see if more will come.*
5. *If there is no more, get some toilet paper.*
6. *We fold the toilet paper (as you show them how).*
7. *We wipe front to back and throw the dirty paper in the toilet.*
8. *We wipe again until the paper comes back clean.*
9. *We pull up our underwear and then our pants.*
10. *We flush the toilet.*
11. *We wash our hands and dry.*

You can mix it up too. One time you can narrate all the various actions yourself, and another time you can narrate parts of it, asking your child:

> "What do you think we do next?"

You can answer the question if they don't know or remember.

THEY POOPED IN THE POTTY

Again, you want to celebrate—this is GREAT! Show your child how incredibly proud of them you are. You might say,

> *"You did it! You pooped in the potty.*
> *You felt the need to poop, and you listened to your body*
> *and put the poop where it goes—in the potty—way to go!"*

Either help your child carry the potty pot with the poop to the big toilet, or you can do it. Then empty it into the toilet. If your child wants, they can flush it away, saying:

> *"Bye-bye, poo-poo."*

If your child does not poop on day one, that's OK. If they have an accident and poop on the floor, think of it as a learning opportunity, and remind them:

> "Oh no, you pooped on the floor. Next time, let's poop in the potty."

DAY 1
STEP-BY-STEP/CONTINUED

Mommy Hack

DRINKING AT NIGHT
If your child demands to have some water at night, offer a very small, shot-glass-size cup that will wet their whistle but minimize the amount of liquid they consume.

NAPTIME

Before your child goes down for their nap, make a trip to the potty and encourage your child to try and go. During naptime, you can put them in a diaper or pull-ups, explaining to them that:

"You will only wear a pull-up during naps and at bedtime. That's because, when you are sleeping, you may not wake up to use the potty. When you do get up from your nap, we will take the pull-up off."

After the nap, we recommend that you take your child to the potty for another attempt at peeing and pooping.

NO MORE DRINKS

After dinner, as bedtime approaches—two hours before going to bed—reduce or avoid giving any liquids to your child.

BEDTIME

Before bedtime, make one last trip to the potty. This should be an extended potty break, so read a book or sing songs—anything that will help extend the time your child is on the potty.

HAVE CLEAR EXPECTATIONS

Daytime potty training is not the same as nighttime potty training. **DON'T** expect that your child will be dry during the night or at naps.

A BIT OF PUSH BACK

While trying to get your child to go to the potty, you may encounter some resistance. Don't worry, it's normal. You are introducing something completely new. It's a change in the normal routine, and toddlers love consistent routines.

Remain calm and carry on. When you have gotten your child to sit on the potty, we encourage parents to work their magic—distraction. Do whatever you can to creatively keep them on the potty, as it typically takes several minutes for a child to relax their pelvic floor to go. Around two to three minutes for a pee and three to five minutes for a poop.

OUR FREE ILLUSTRATED POTTY CHART

Scan the QR code to easily get our step-by-step illustrated potty chart. Perfect to hang up in your bathroom for your child to follow.

DAY 2
ONE DOWN—ONWARD

During day two, you will continue to follow the same steps
as on day one. Essentially these days are an opportunity to practice
what your child has learned thus far.

QUICK TIP

It can be helpful to
have a portable potty with bags
in your car, so that when you
are out and about and your
child needs to go, they can
use the
portable potty.

DAY TWO

Day two is basically the same as day one. It's important to be consistent and
maintain the routine established on day one, including frequent potty breaks.

During day one, your child may be either completely naked or just
bare bottom wearing only a shirt/top. Toward the end of day two, if things
are progressing well and your child is consistently peeing and pooping in
the potty, you either may introduce underwear or you can wait until day
three to introduce them.

TRANSITIONING TO UNDERWEAR

Now is the time your child gets to try out the incredibly cool
character underwear that you picked out together.
You can say:

*"You have been doing such a great job getting
your pee and poop in the potty. It's time to try out your
new super cool underwear."*

You can also say:

"Be sure to keep your (character name) dry. They don't like to be wet."

*"Make sure you don't pee on _____ (character name).
_____ (Character name) will not like that."*

TRANSITIONING TO UNDERWEAR CONTINUED

NOTE: Transitioning to underwear is an important step in training and has several benefits:

1. Underwear, unlike a diaper or pull-up, allows your child to feel that they are wet, which helps them understand that they have had an accident.
2. Many children do not like the feeling of being wet, so underwear can help motivate them to go to the potty to stay dry.
3. Wearing underwear provides a child the opportunity to practice pulling clothing up and down, which is a key skill necessary to successfully using the potty.

When your child has an accident, resist the urge to immediately change them into clean underwear.

While you don't want to leave your child in dirty underwear, you do want your child to learn that wetting their underwear or pants is unpleasant and something they will want to avoid.

Allowing them time to be in the wet underwear gives your child time to realize they had an accident. This may only be a couple minutes before you change them. When that happens, take them to the bathroom to change them, saying:

" We don't pee or poop in our underwear/pants. That doesn't feel so great, does it? Pee and poo go in the potty."

"Oh, it looks like you had an accident. Gosh, that must not feel so nice. Let's get you changed. Next time, let's try and get the pee in the potty where it belongs."

However, If they pooped in their underwear, then you will want to change them right away. Ideally, you want your child to notice that they had an accident and to tell you so.

DAY 3 & AFTER
WHAT NOW?

During day three, you will continue to reinforce and practice what your child has learned during days one and two.

QUICK TIP

Once your child starts to wear underwear, you will want to make sure that the clothing you put on your child is easy to remove. Elastic waistband pants work best for this.

DAY THREE

Day three, in many ways, is very similar to days one and two. Its focus is on locking in the new skills your child has acquired.

You will:

Provide Continued Reinforcement

Reinforce positive behavior, and continue to be consistent. Keep an eye on your child, and prompt or take them to the potty on your regular potty break schedule.

Celebrate Success

Continue to praise your child for their progress made during the three days.

Refine Independence Skills

As your child becomes more comfortable with using the potty, gradually give them more autonomy in the process. Encourage them to recognize when they need to use the potty and to take the initiative in going independently. Continue refining their skills, for example, wiping and handwashing.

Address Challenges

Be prepared to address any challenges or setbacks that arise during potty training. Stay patient and calm, and provide reassurance and support to help your child overcome difficulties.

AFTER DAY THREE

After three days of training—what happens next?

Your child may be going back to more of their normal routine. It is important to understand that although your child may get the basics of using the potty, it will take several additional weeks for the training to lock in. You may introduce pants or a dress during this time.

Maintain Consistency

Continue a consistent potty routine to reinforce the learned behavior.

Be Patient

Understand that accidents may still occur. Be patient and supportive throughout the journey. After your child has mastered potty training, continue to offer support and encouragement as needed.

Potty Breaks

Depending on how your child is doing, you may again extend the time between potty breaks.

Encourage Independence

Check out the "I Do It!" spread on pages 103–104 for how to foster greater pottying independence in your child.

Mommy Hack

During training, it is very helpful to learn your child's pee pattern to understand how often and when your child typically needs to pee. This will help you know when to plan to take your child to the potty.

THE SIMPLEST METHOD

AT-A-GLANCE METHOD OVERVIEW

Your quick view cheat sheet for the various steps of the Simplest Potty Training method.

QUICK VIEW—STEP BY STEP

- After all the months of preparation, you are ready to get started.
- Keep the potty in the same spot it's been in so your child knows where it is.
- Set aside three days to stay home during the initial active training. A whole week is even better if you can manage it.
- No appointments, cell phones, social media. Focus 100 percent on your child's training.
- Eat a good breakfast, with lots of liquids and fiber.
- Together, collect and give away all diapers/pull-ups. No going back now.
- Start training with your toddler naked or bare bottom from the waist down.
- Let them run around nude/commando for two to three days in the designated area.
- Have them drink more liquids than normal so they have lots of opportunities to pee.
- Follow your potty break schedule. Setting a timer will help you stay on schedule.
- Narrate the process as you go.
- Wash hands at every attempt, whether or not they pee or poop in the potty.
- Let your child master going to the potty naked before putting on underwear or pants.
- Transition to underwear.
- When adding underwear and pants, they should be loose fitting, easy off and on.
- When things get challenging, don't put a diaper or pull-up back on.
- There will be a few rough days, but stay strong, committed, and consistent.
- Big, happy celebrations. Lots of praise when your child successfully uses the potty.
- If nothing comes out after a few minutes on the potty, don't force it. Try again later.
- Mark the potty chart with stickers for successes, and, if using them, reward your child.
- Have the child help clean up their messes (just pee, not poop).
- Follow the nap and bedtime ritual.
- Inform the teachers at school/day care, so they can help, as they are experts.

OUT & ABOUT
TIME TO TAKE A BREAK

The first three days of potty training can be really rough, staying home and just watching your child. Here is what to know if you decide to change things up.

VENTURING OUT

Some people choose to leave their home for short periods to break things up a bit. Ideally, we recommend you **DON'T** take your child out—and that you stay at home and focus on training. Different environments can only make training harder.

If you feel you want get out of the house, do so right after an extended potty attempt. We suggest that you make the outing **SHORT** so you can return home before your child needs to go again.

We know that going out while potty training can be stressful, and it's tempting to want to put a pull-up or diaper on your little one. DON'T DO IT!

Putting a pull-up or diaper on now sends your little one mixed messages and is likely to cause a setback in their training.

Mommy Hack

When venturing out, it can be helpful if you make a pottying attempt before you leave and upon arriving at your destination, whether it be at the store, at school, or at any restaurant.

TIPS AND ADVICE

POTTY BREAK

Before you leave home, be sure to make a trip to the potty so your child can try to go.

KEEP IT SHORT

Any outing should be short—no long or extended journeys. It is helpful to do some test runs, for example, by arranging outings to friends' houses where you can have a little bit more control. NO errands, like grocery shopping, or anything requiring a long drive. Outings should be quick and brief.

GET PACKING

Be sure you have your go bag with everything you might need for the potty and for accidents if they occur. Bring a good, quality portable travel potty with you.

LIMIT THE DRINKS

For these brief outings, hold off on the liquids until you are back home.

CHANGE OF CLOTHING

Pack a couple of changes of clothing for your child and for you too.

PIT STOPS

Be prepared to make several visits to the toilet, and stick to your scheduled times for potty breaks. Consistency is important. You can set a timer to help remind yourself when to take your child to the potty.

PLAN IT OUT

If you choose to venture out, know ahead of time where the toilets are.

HELLO, TRAVEL POTTY

It helps to introduce the travel potty at home so your child is familiar with it and has used it ahead of time.

WASH UP
TEACHING HANDWASHING

You may have already introduced your child to washing their hands, but if not, it's time. Those little hands are likely going to get pee and poop on them.

Mommy Hack

A great way to introduce handwashing to your child is by reading them one of the very cute children's books about washing hands and getting rid of germs.

STEPS FOR TEACHING HANDWASHING

STEP 1: STEP UP

You will more than likely need a step stool so your toddler can reach the sink. First, help your toddler step up on the stool so that they can reach the faucet.

STEP 2: WET YOUR TODDLERS' HANDS

Explain how the faucet works: one is for cold water, and the other for hot. Explain that they need to be careful so that the water is not too hot. Then, help your toddler wet their hands by putting them in the warm water.

STEP 3: ADD SOAP

Show your toddler how to use the liquid or bar soap, and how, by rubbing their hands together, they can make bubbles, saying, "Let's see the bubbles."

STEP 4: SCRUB FOR 20 SECONDS

Have your toddler take their time, and show them how to clean their palms, the backs of their hands, in between their fingers, and under their nails. The Center for Disease Control (CDC) recommends you wash hands for 20 seconds.

STEP 5: RINSE

Using lukewarm water, help your child rinse off the soap and dirt.

STEP 6: DRY

Using a clean, dry towel, show your child how to dry their hands, and then return the towel to the rack when they are done. If using paper towels, show them how to take a small quantity to dry their hands.

TALK ABOUT IT

While you help your toddler wash their hands, be sure to explain each step and tell them how important it is to wash their hands every time they use the potty to get rid of germs and to keep from getting sick.

"Let's get rid of those yucky germs."

QUICK TIP

How long is 20 seconds?

Singing either Twinkle, Twinkle Little Star or Mary Had a Little Lamb once, or Happy Birthday twice, takes about 20 seconds.

GET YOUR FREE HANDWASHING CHART

Scan the QR code to get our free handwashing chart. It can help your child remember the correct steps for washing their hands.

TOILET PAPER
TEACHING HOW TO USE IT

How to use toilet paper may seem like it needs no explanation, but when you've never done it, well, there are some things to learn.

OVERVIEW

You have accomplished the big one—your child is sitting on the potty and peeing and pooping. Now you need to teach them how to wipe/clean themselves. Learning to wipe their tushy is a developmental skill, and this process may take a bit of time before your child is able to correctly and completely wipe themselves clean.

So, you will be the official wiper for a while, as your little one can't see back there very well and may not be able to reach behind themselves.

Even though you may not expect them to wipe themselves to start, you can begin laying the groundwork for using toilet paper by walking them through the steps as you help them.

QUICK TIP

Teach your child to wipe **FRONT** to **BACK**

This is especially important for girls because it helps to prevent Urinary Tract Infections (UTIs) and for good hygiene. For boys, this is less of an issue.

Mommy Hack

Your child is just learning how wiping works, and, as they do, they will likely be using **A LOT** of toilet paper. It is best to monitor their efforts to prevent them from using too much toilet paper and clogging up the toilet.

Painter's Tape

One trick for getting just the right amount of toilet paper is to put a mark on the wall with a character Band-Aid or some painter's tape to indicate how far your child should roll out the toilet paper to get just the right amount.

HOW TO USE TOILET PAPER & WIPE CLEAN

LEAD BY EXAMPLE

When you go to the bathroom, bring your child and let them see what you do when you go poop. Show them the various steps, from pulling a certain amount of toilet paper to folding it and wiping yourself to refolding and rewiping until the toilet paper comes back clean after wiping.

We know it can be a bit awkward, even embarrassing for some parents, but actually letting your child see what you are doing as you are doing it can be very helpful.

THE RIGHT AMOUNT

Show your child how to unroll the toilet paper using just four squares. Another method that some day care facilities use is teaching children to wrap their hand twice with toilet paper to get the right amount.

PRACTICE FOLDING

Show your child how to fold the toilet paper, and practice holding the toilet paper flat across their fingers, securing it with their thumb. Then, with your hand lightly over theirs, help them wipe. Show your child how to reach behind and target the proper area and wipe themselves from front to back.

Then show them how to take the dirty toilet paper and fold it over to a clean area to use to wipe again. For some children, the folding to wipe again may be too difficult. If so, skip that part and just have them get another four squares of toilet paper.

WIPE UNTIL CLEAN

Show your child how to wipe, then look at the paper, and if dirty, fold it again or get four new squares of toilet paper and rewipe until the toilet paper comes back clean. Throw the dirty toilet paper in the big toilet.

PRACTICE FLUSHING

You will want to show your child how to pull the handle down or push the button and release it to flush the toilet.

NARRATE THE PROCESS

Throughout the process, narrate everything you do. Don't hesitate to overshare, and repeat yourself each time your child goes to the bathroom.

CHART IT
CHARTS & REWARDS OVERVIEW

Some people swear by them, while others have concerns.
Here is how charts and rewards generally work.

Mommy Hack

KEEPING AN EYE ON THE PRIZE

Sometimes it can be even more motivating if your child knows what the prizes are, so putting them in a jar next to the potty can help.

WHAT IS IT?
POTTY TRAINING CHART

Charts are used to track, reward, and encourage a child's peeing and/or pooping successes.

HOW IT WORKS

There are different ways to use a potty training chart, but the most common way is to mark the chart with a sticker or check mark after each successful trip to the potty. Success is defined by peeing or pooping even a little in the potty. Once your child has reached a certain number of stickers, they potentially can earn a small prize/reward.

A reward can be received for:

1. Successfully peeing or pooping in the potty.
2. Earning a certain number of success stickers or stars.

WHAT TO DO FIRST
GET A CHART

Find a chart that is right for you and your child. There are several types of charts available online for free or to purchase. You can make you own, or you can download our FREE Simplest potty charts.

FIND THE RIGHT STICKERS

Stickers can range from your child's favorite characters to simple stars, etc.

DETERMINE THE REWARD

Some people use candy or a small toy, while others let the stickers be the reward itself. Every child is different and what motivates one may not work for another. You will need to determine what type of reward works best for you and your child.

INTRODUCE THE CHART

Explain the potty chart to your child in easy-to-understand language. Tell them what will happen and the exciting little surprises that they will receive when they achieve the specific task or goal.

PLACE THE CHART

Place your chart in a highly visible location where your child will see it. This can be a great way to remind them to try and use the potty.

HOORAY

Celebrate and make a big deal out of your child's successful attempts on the potty. Be super positive and tell your child how proud you are that they used the potty.

MARK THE CHART

Upon your child's success, let them place the sticker on the chart. As they put their sticker on the chart, you will reinforce their success by telling your child that they are only (x many) stickers or stars away from getting a prize.

TIMELY REWARDS

Whether stickers, treats, or praise, any reward or positive reinforcement should be given as soon as the desired behavior is accomplished.

CONS

There are concerns and questions as to whether using a chart/reward system with young children is a good idea. Some believe doing so:
- Reinforces bad food habits if sweets or junk food is the reward.
- Can result in regression once the rewards stops.
- May not work well with young children, as they can't truly grasp delayed gratification.
- May create the need to increase the reward in order to have the same effect again and again, because children can become bored with the same reward.

NOTE: It's important to remember that every child is different, and it is up to each parent to determine if the chart/reward system is right for them and their child. **If you choose to give small treats or toys, you must be careful, because some are potential choking hazards.**

THE SIMPLEST
POTTY-CHART METHOD

We have created our own potty charts that not only reward your child's successes but make a fun game of it. Here is how it works.

SIMPLEST RECOMMENDATIONS

POTTY TRAINING CHART

Using a potty chart is a great way to support the potty learning process. Charts and rewards can work well, as they reinforce a child's understanding of what is expected of them and can help motivate them to learn their new pottying behavior.

REWARDS

At Simplest we recommend **NOT** using candy and toys as rewards every time your child pees or poops.

While toys and candy can be helpful, we believe, if given every single time your child pees or poops, they potentially can create other issues. Here is why:

Kids tend to get bored with getting just one M&M or piece of candy every time they pee or poop and soon may require several pieces in order to have the same level of motivation. The same is true of toys. Children will typically want to get more or bigger toys for the same results.

Children can be rather clever, and you might find your child is deliberately peeing just a little bit to get some candy in order to come back a little later to pee just a little more to get more candy—essentially gaming the system.

We recommend the rewards be a combination of several things. First and foremost, your personal praise, then a sticker that your child gets to put on the chart indicating a success, and finally, a reward after achieving X number of successes.

HOW IT WORKS

THEY PEED IN THE POTTY

When your child successfully pees in the potty, this is what we recommend you do:

PRAISE, PRAISE, PRAISE

Hooray! This is super exciting, and you should let your child know how thrilled and proud you are of them.

"You did it. You peed in the potty!
You felt the need to pee, and you listened to your body
and put the pee where it belongs—in the potty. Hooray!"

STICKER TIME

Your child can pick one sticker, which they get to place on the potty chart.

"You got a sticker. Hooray!
Let's put the sticker on the chart and help _____ get to
_____."

THEY POOPED IN THE POTTY

When you child successfully poops in the potty, here is what you should do:

PRAISE, PRAISE, PRAISE

Just like peeing, you want to let your child know how happy you are for what they have accomplished. You might say:

"Wow, you pooped in the potty. You did a great job!
I'm sooooooo proud of you."

STICKER TIME

Your child can pick two stickers that they get to place on the chart.

"You got two stickers—way to go!
Let's put these stickers on the chart and help _____ get to
_____."

GAME ON
THE SIMPLEST POTTY CHART METHOD

THE SIMPLEST POTTY CHARTS

The Simplest potty charts not only track the success of your child but make a bit of a game of it. Kids can get more invested in trying to help their character reach a goal than by solely tracking their own performance.

Children learn <u>BEST</u> through play.

HOW THEY WORK

Choose a theme or character that your child likes. We suggest showing your child the chart options on the next page and letting them pick one.

- **Fairy Princess** (child's name) is missing the cupcake for her princess tea party and needs your help finding it.
- **Magic Unicorn** (child's name) is losing her magic and needs to get to the magic cupcakes to recharge her rainbow magic power.
- (Child's name), **the Monster Truck** wants to win the candy cup trophy but needs your help getting to it.
- (Child's name), **the Dinosaur** loves cake and cookies and needs your help getting to some yummy cookies.

One Sticker

Every time your child pees in the potty, they get one sticker, which, when put on the chart, moves the character closer to what they want or need.

Two Stickers

Every time your child poops in the potty, they get two stickers, which moves the character two spaces closer to what the character is trying to get to.

Every now and again, in a fun, upbeat voice, explain how the character is getting closer to getting to the goal and that your child is doing a great job helping them. Tell them that they should keep up the good work and soon the character and your child will get the reward, a piece of candy, cookie, or something your toddler likes.

FREE STICKER CHARTS

GET OUR FREE STICKER POTTY CHART!

Scan the QR code to easily get the FREE Simplest potty chart.

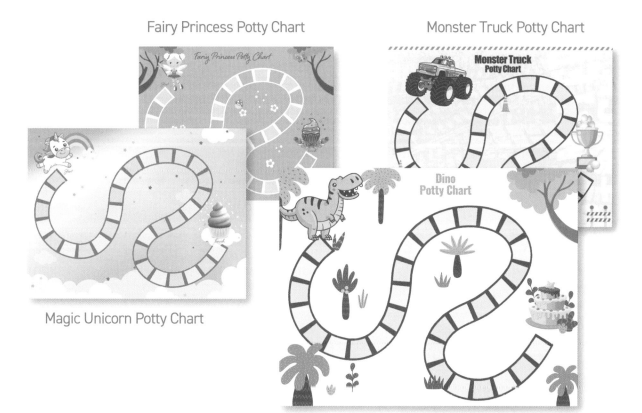

Fairy Princess Potty Chart

Monster Truck Potty Chart

Magic Unicorn Potty Chart

Dinosaur Potty Chart

EXAMPLE: MAX THE DINOSAUR

STORY/HOW IT WORKS

Max the Dinosaur is super hungry and Max LOOOOVES cookies. He sees his favorite cookies at the end of the path, but he can't get to them—oh no! Max really needs your help reaching them. Every time you pee or poop in the potty you get a sticker to put on the chart. The stickers show the way to go so Max can follow your stickers and to get to those yummy cookies.

NOTE: If you choose to give small treats or toys, you must be careful, because some can be potential choking hazards.

OOPS!
THERE WILL BE ACCIDENTS

Let's face it, accidents are a normal part of potty training, so you should expect that there will be many oops moments.

NOW WHAT?

Okay—so it happened! Stay calm and center yourself. There are several ways you might approach handling the accident.

*"Looks like you had an accident.
Let's go to the bathroom and get you changed."*

*"I noticed that you were
(<u>what your child is doing</u>), and you forgot
to go to the bathroom
and had an accident. Next time you feel
you need to go, let's stop what you are doing
and go to the potty."*

*"Next time you feel like you have to go,
let's hurry up and go to the
potty, so you can quickly get back
to (<u>whatever your child was doing</u>) and
don't have an accident."*

TIPS FOR DEALING WITH ACCIDENTS

ABSOLUTELY NO PUNISHMENT

You should **NOT** yell at or discipline your child for having an accident. This accomplishes nothing and can make the problem worse. Be sure your tone of of voice and what you say are positive and encouraging.

STAY CALM

Keep cool and don't get stressed out. Your stress can cause your child to become stressed as well.

SET A SCHEDULE

Follow a set schedule where you take your child to the bathroom according to your potty break schedule, and have them try to go even if they say they don't need to.

SLOW IT DOWN

Encourage your child to take their time when going to the bathroom and fully empty their bladder. It helps if you sit with them while they are on the potty.

NOTE IT

If your child is continually having accidents at school, it might be wise to send a note to school asking that your child be allowed to go to the bathroom anytime they need to go.

CHANGE OF CLOTHING

Be sure to send a couple changes of clothes to school or day care just in case there is an accident. You will also want to have a change of clothes for your child in the car, just in case.

GO BEFORE YOU GO

Encourage your child to try and use the bathroom before you leave the house—even if they say they don't have to.

WHERE'S THE POOP?

HOLDING THE POOP

When you begin potty training, you might notice that your child, who normally has been pooping two to three times a day, is now pooping less. What is going on?

WHAT IS GOING ON HERE?

It is not unusual for a little one, who, while wearing diapers, might poop two to three times a day, to suddenly stop pooping now that the diaper is gone. If it has not stopped entirely, it might have slowed down considerably.

Not to worry, this is completely normal. Remember that since your child was an infant, they have pooped and peed only in a diaper. Now that the diaper is gone, they are experiencing a very different sensation, which might cause them to hesitate when they need to have a bowel movement.

While it is not unusual for kids who are beginning potty training to have fewer poos, you should keep an eye on this so that your child does not become constipated. This can happen if a child holds the poop in for too long. It also can result in additional complications for potty training. Check out the spread on "Constipation," pages 133–34.

TIPS FOR KEEPING THINGS MOVING

WATCH THE DIET

It can be helpful to make sure your child has a diet that is high in fiber. This will keep things moving to avoid your child becoming constipated.

They can eat:

Whole Grains

| Bran Cereal | Oatmeal | Wheat Bread |

Legumes

| Beans | Lentils | Chickpeas |

Fruits

| Apples | Oranges | Berries |
| Pears | Mangoes | Peaches |

Vegetables

Peas	Carrots	Broccoli
Brussels Sprouts	Greens	Avocados
Sweet Potatoes		

STAYING HYDRATED

Make sure your child is well hydrated by giving them plenty of fluids (water, milk, etc.).

GET MOVING

Encouraging your child to be active can help the bowels get moving too.

TIPS
A LITTLE HELPFUL RECAP

A few more practical suggestions that can help the training go smoothly and reduce your family's stress levels.

Mommy Hack

During training it is best to choose clothing that is easy on and easy off. Avoid pants with buttons or clasps that are difficult to remove to help prevent unfortunate accidents.

IT WILL GO SIDEWAYS

At some point you may feel that everything is going wrong. This often happens during the second and third days. Don't throw in the towel right away. Continue to stick with it. Many times the resistance or issue will resolve itself if you continue to move ahead with training.

TIPS

PREPARE YOUR CHILD

Walking your child through the process ahead of time is critically important. Children love to know what is going to happen next.

PREPARE YOURSELF

Potty training can be pretty intense for parents, too, so it is wise to prepare yourself mentally before beginning.

GO BEFORE YOU GO

If you are planning on leaving your house during training, have your child use the potty before you go, and try again once you arrive at your destination.

BE SUPPORTIVE

For some children, the feeling of not wearing a diaper can be scary and uncomfortable. They will look to you for reassurance, so remain calm.

DON'T GET DISCOURAGED

It can be very easy to get discouraged on day two when your child is having accidents. Stay calm, positive, and patient.

PRAISE, PRAISE, PRAISE

Shower your child with tons of praise every time they are successful or use rewards to help motivate them to get it right.

PLAN MEALS

As you will be super focused on your child during the first days of training, planning ahead for how you will handle meals can be helpful. Preparing meals before starting training and having a supply of easy-to-prepare frozen foods can also help. In a pinch, you can always order in.

PROTECT THE FURNITURE

Consider protecting any furniture in the area where you are confining your child, so it is not peed on. Consider putting leakproof covers over them.

CONTROL THE TEMP

As your child is going to potentially be bare bottom or naked, make sure the temperature in your home is warm enough for your child.

THEY WANT A DIAPER

If your child wants their diapers back during training, you can remind them that they are all gone.

QUICK TIP

"If you've got to go, let me know."

Ask, ask, ask. Using some phrase to continually ask if your child needs to go can be very helpful.

Keep up
the good
work.

SUSTAIN

Your child has successfully shown they know how to use the potty. Now you want to lock in what they have learned for continued pottying success.

THE MUST-HAVES
FOR OUT & ABOUT

GET THE RIGHT STUFF!
Scan the QR code to easily get our recommendations for all the essentials you will need when you and your child are out and about.

1 PORTABLE POTTY
When looking for a standalone travel potty, make sure it has stable, foldable legs. It's a plus if it has nonslip grips on the feet. It should have an easy-to-clean basin or easy-to-fit liners to catch pee and poo. Ideally, it comes with its own travel bag. We also recommend it have a splash guard.

8–10 BIG BOY OR GIRL UNDERWEAR
Look for underwear made of breathable material, like cotton or bamboo. They should fit snuggly but not be too tight.

FLUSHABLE WET WIPES
Wipes should be hypoallergenic, biodegradable, unscented, and fragrance- and paraben-free.

2–3 CHANGES OF CLOTHING
Accidents are a part of potty training, so it is wise to carry with you an extra set of clothing (including underwear, pants, shirt, socks, and shoes) for you and your child when those "oh no" moments occur.

1–2 TOILET SEAT REDUCERS
Look for a contoured seat that fits snuggly inside the full-size toilet seat. It should be stable and nonslip, easy to clean, and have a handle or hook for storage. Made of BPA-free plastics.

HAND SANITIZER

Sanitizer should be 60 to 95 percent alcohol and be free of parabens, PEGs (polyethylene glycol), and fragrances. Avoid products that use artificial colors or dyes.

2 WET BAGS | GARBAGE BAGS

These reusable, zippered bags should be leakproof, waterproof, and able to prevent odors from escaping with a good, quality zipper closure.

STICKY NOTES/PAINTER'S TAPE

Ideally, these sticky notes should be three-by-three inches—so that they easily cover the toilet sensor—and made from recycled or recyclable paper. They should be sticky but not so sticky that they damage or leave a residue on any surface when removed. Painter's tape is also a clever option for covering the flushing sensor.

2–3 PULL-UPS

Just for emergencies, it is wise to have them with you. These should be highly absorbent to contain pee and poop, with a wetness indicator. They should have waistbands and leg bands with some stretchability. They should be phthalate-, paraben-, bisphenol-, formaldehyde-, and fragrance-free.

2–3 EXTRA TOWELS

It is wise to have a few towels in the car just in case a potty accident happens while you are out. You also might want to have a small and a large towel made from high-quality materials, such as 100 percent combed cotton, bamboo, or a blend of natural fibers.

CONTINUED PROGRESS
REINFORCING THE TRAINING

If your child has a handle on recognizing when they need to pee or poop and lets you know when they have to go, it's time to work on locking these good habits in.

STAY ON COURSE

You have made really great progress getting to this point with your child. Continue to utilize the techniques from the practice phase of training as you keep working with your child. Now is not the time to back off or stop providing positive reinforcement—just the opposite.

GREAT JOB!

Continue to provide tons of praise and support. Rewarding their successes and encouraging your child will reinforce their progress.

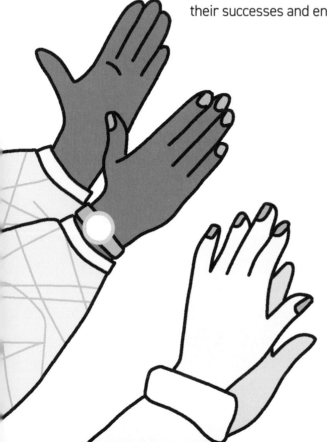

WHAT REINFORCEMENT DOES

Positive reinforcement is the acknowledgment and rewarding of your child for a positive behavior, thereby increasing the likelihood that the behavior becomes more automatic—until they are doing it all on their own.

BENEFITS

As your child continues to build on their earlier successes, the positive reinforcement not only helps your child achieve pottying success but also:

- Builds greater confidence.
- Enhances self-esteem in your child.
- Promotes greater independence.
- Fosters bonding and a positive relationship with you.
- Reduces overall stress for both you and your child.
- Helps motivate and keep your child engaged.
- Establishes good habits.

KEEP UP THE
GOOD WORK!

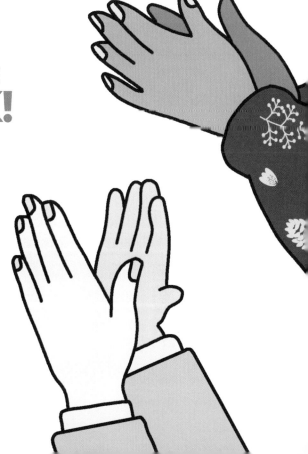

I DO IT!
MOVING TOWARD TOILETING INDEPENDENCE

How to encourage your child to use the potty without you.

WHAT TO KNOW

Many preschool children are expected to be able to go to the bathroom on their own. For this reason, you will not only need to potty train your child but you will also need to foster and teach them to be able to do it on their own.

GO SLOW

It is important to understand that developing pottying independence is a process and takes time, so be patient, and don't try and rush it.

PRAISE

Just as when you where teaching your child how to use the potty, you should encourage pottying independence by praising them when they do any part of the pottying process themselves.

GET YOUR <u>FREE</u> PROCESS CHARTS

Scan the QR code to easily get our illustrated chart for how to use the potty and how to wash hands.

TIPS TO FOSTER INDEPENDENCE

CLEAR A PATH

Make sure that the path to the bathroom at home is clear of any obstacles that might obstruct them en route to the potty.

EVERYTHING IN ITS PLACE

Make sure that everything—the stool, toilet insert, soap, towels, etc.—your child needs for pottying is always in the same place and easy for them to get and use on their own.

DRESS FOR SUCCESS

Make sure that the clothing your child is wearing can be snapped, zipped, or buttoned by them. Consider using pants with elastic waists, which are much easier for little ones to manage.

STEP BY STEP

Once your child knows how to do each of the pottying steps, you can start developing pottying independence. After your child has peed, pooped, wiped, dressed, and has begun washing their hands, you can step outside or partly step outside of the room before they are finished. You will be on standby if they need you. By doing this, they will begin to learn that you don't need to be there all the time. If needed, reassure your child that you are right there ready to help them.

PRIVACY PLEASSSSEEEE

You can start to teach your child about privacy while they are learning how to use the potty by closing the door or leaving it just slightly ajar while they are going. This will get them in the habit of partly shutting the door while going.

At first you will not want your toddler to completely shut the door so you can keep an eye on them and help them when needed. Not having them shut the door completely can help prevent them from accidentally locking themselves in the bathroom.

PICTURE THIS

If your child has a hard time remembering the steps to pottying and washing their hands, you can attach to the wall an illustrated printout of what to do. Use the QR code on page 103.

TO-GO BAG
WHAT TO PACK DURING TRAINING

Now that you are potty training, there are a few things we suggest you add to your on-the-go bag. Here is what you will need.

OVERVIEW

Leaving home while you are potty training can be nerve-racking and stressful, so being poo- and pee-pared is important. We have put together a list of the on-the-go bag essentials that will help you deal with all the various challenges that might come up.

FREE DOWNLOAD

Scan the QR code to get a list of recommendations for the essentials a well-prepared potty training on-the-go bag should include.

QUICK TIP

Before going out with your child and upon arriving at your destination, it is wise to head straight to the bathroom to make an attempt to pee and poop.

PACKING A POTTY TRAINING TO-GO BAG

2–3 PULL-UPS:
Have a few extra pull-ups in
case of emergency.

2 CHANGES OF CLOTHES
Accidents will happen, so you
will need to be prepared with a
change of clothing: underwear,
pants, shirt, shorts, and socks.

2–3 PLASTIC BAGS
Plastic bags or a wet/dry bag
for soiled clothing when those
accidents occur.

WET WIPES
Hypoallergenic, fragrance-free,
flushable wipes.

1 TRAVEL POTTY
You will want to invest in a
travel potty, either a toilet seat
insert or portable potty.

HAND SANITIZER
Sanitizer that is 60 to 95 percent
alcohol and parabens-, PEGs-,
and fragrance-free.

SUNSCREEN
Broad-spectrum protection
that is water resistant and made
from nontoxic ingredients.

KIDS' UTENSILS
A children's spoon and fork.

SMALL TOYS
Small toys to entertain your
little one.

KIDS' MEDICATION
Children's pain medicine,
like Paracetamol or Ibuprofen
(consult your doctor).

FIRST-AID KIT
Band-Aids, Neosporin, child-safe
bug spray.

EMERGENCY INFO
It is wise to have your doctor's,
your partner's, and your contact
info handy.

A HAT
Bring a child's hat to protect
their head from the sun.

1 SIPPY CUP
It should be leakproof and made
from BPA-free plastic.

HAIR SUPPLIES
Extra hair bands and a travel-size
brush are a good idea.

SNACKS
Typical snacks as well as reward
treats for when pee or poo goes in
the potty.

CHANGING PAD
Waterproof and cushioned that
folds up easily.

STICKY NOTES
If your child is freaked out by the
automated flush of public toilets,
you can cover the sensor with a
sticky note or painter's tape.

CHANGE OF CLOTHING FOR YOU
Maybe not for the diaper bag, but something you definitely want to have with you is a change of
clothing—a full change of clothing—including underwear (JUST IN CASE).

DAY CARE

IT'S A TEAM EFFORT

Individual day care facilities have a wide range of policies regarding potty training. Here is what you need to know.

QUICK TIP

Coordinate with your day care or preschool how potty training will be handled, and then repeatedly share this with your child so they know what will happen at their day care or preschool.

DAY CARE—WHAT TO KNOW

Some day cares require a child to wear pull-ups until they are sure that the child is fully trained, while others require that children be fully trained before they can attend, and still others will let children wear only underwear during their training.

It is best to check with your chosen day care to understand their policy concerning potty training before you begin training. These policies typically cannot be changed and usually are in place for legal and hygienic reasons.

TIPS FOR DAY CARE POTTY TRAINING

It is important to speak with your day care before you begin potty training to:

- **Understand their policies.**
- **Engage them in the training.**
- **Ensure consistency at home and at day care.**
- **Understand how they handle accidents.**

If you are using a specific technique to potty train your child, you should share that with the day care provider to see if they are willing and able to continue the training using that technique.

Your child will have accidents, so letting your child know that they may happen and how the caregivers will handle them at school is important. This will help ease any anxiety and fear your child may experience when an accident occurs.

The key to successful potty training at day care is
open communication & consistency.

It is important to share with your day care anything that will help them with potty training your child. If there are particular signs that your child shows when they need to go potty, share them.

Make sure you and the day care are aligned on a plan and what will happen at school. Then speak with your child about going potty at school and what will happen before they return to school. Part of that conversation could look like this:

> *"You have done such a good job at using the potty and letting me know when you need to pee or poop at home. Now you will be using the potty at school. You will need to tell your teacher when you need to pee and poop."*

On the first day back, you should have a conversation with your child and the teacher, reinforcing what will go on and how the teacher will be helping your child.

Mommy Hack

Be sure to bring extra pants, underwear, shirt, and socks to the day care or preschool so everyone is prepared in case there is an accident, and trust me, there will be accidents.

NOTE: It can be helpful when you drop off your child at day care to go straight to the bathroom and try to go. You might also consider having your child try and go before you leave to take them home at the end of the day.

FROM POTTY TO TOILET
HOW TO TRANSITION TO THE BIG TOILET

You have trained your child using a potty chair, and now your child is ready to trade in the child-size potty for the full-size toilet. Although you may not think it's a big deal, it can be for your child.

OVERVIEW

A full-size toilet can be scary for a little ones. It's common for them to be afraid of falling in, so it's important to make sure your child is ready for the transition and feels at ease and safe. Don't try to rush the process. Let your child lead the way.

WHEN TO TRANSITION

Each child is different and will progress as they are ready. You should guide and prompt your child to use the toilet, but if they don't wish to, don't force it.

TIPS TO EASE THE TRANSITION

GO SLOW

If it is not there already, move the potty chair to the bathroom.

LEAD BY EXAMPLE

Let your child watch you or a family member use the toilet— the whole process from start to finish.

GET A TOILET INSERT

Your little one is smaller than the toilet seat's opening, so you will need a toddler-size seat insert that fits on top of the full-size toilet seat. It should be sturdy and fit securely.

GET A STEP STOOL

Full-size toilets are taller than the potty chair, and your child will need a stool to get up onto the toilet seat. Your child can also use the stool to rest and slightly elevate their feet while going pee and poop.

QUICK TIP

Every child is different. There is no set time for when to transition from a potty to the big toilet.

DON'T FORCE IT!
Depending on the age of your child, let your child lead the transition.

Mommy Hack

Be sure to sit with your child as they begin to learn how to use the big toilet. You can hold their legs or thighs to help them feel more secure and prevent them from feeling they will fall into the toilet.

TAKE A SEAT
MOUNTING THE BIG TOILET

Your child is transitioning to the big toilet—what's the best way to teach your child to take their pants down, climb onto the stool, and take a seat?

OVERVIEW

Climbing onto the big toilet is no small feat for a little one. Whether or not you are using a toilet seat reducer, it takes some balancing for your child to get seated properly. You will want to provide lots of support as your child learns how to do it.

UP-FRONT TIPS

Talk It Up

While your child is still mastering the basics of potty training, it helps to begin preparing your child for the big toilet by talking about how big boys and girls use the big toilet just like parents do.

Seat Reducer

If you can, leave the toilet seat reducer in the toilet seat, so it is ready for your child to use.

Clothing

You might want to make sure that the clothing your child is wearing is something they can easily remove.

Don't Rush

Change can be scary, so go slow.

Make It Fun

You can make the big toilet more fun for your child by letting them decorate the lid with removable stickers.

QUICK TIP

Although it would be wonderful if your child completed all the steps perfectly right away, it's not likely. Expect that you will need to continue to help your child for a while until they really get the hang of it.

STEPS FOR MOUNTING THE TOILET

PLACE THE POTTY

If you have not done so already, place the potty in the bathroom.

PLACE THE SEAT REDUCER

If you are using a toilet seat reducer, make sure they know how to place it securely in the toilet seat.

STEP UP

Teach your child to step up onto the top step of the stool and turn around with their thighs resting against the toilet for stability.

TAKE PANTS DOWN

Begin by helping them pull down their pants and underwear while they are standing on the stool. Ultimately, they will be doing this themselves.

STEP DOWN

Show them how to carefully get off the toilet using the step stool.

WIPE

Show them how to wipe themselves, but you will more than likely still be wiping your child for a while. Once wiped, show them how to throw the dirty toilet paper into the toilet.

PULLING UP PANTS

The next step is to teach them how to pull up their underwear and pants.

FLUSH

Finally, show them how to flush the toilet.

BOYS' PEEING
SHOULD I SIT OR SHOULD I STAND?

Although boys can sit or stand to pee, we strongly suggest that you first start potty training with sitting down. Once your son has mastered peeing while sitting, then you can move on to learning to pee standing up.

IS HE READY?

The first thing to do is decide if your son is ready to learn to pee standing up. Here are some questions that will help you determine his readiness.

- While standing on the ground, does your son's penis reach the toilet bowl?
- Is your son rather independent and focused?
- Can he pull his pants and underwear down and up?
- Can he lift the toilet lid and seat and put them back down by himself?
- Is he coordinated enough to keep his pee in the toilet?

YOU NEED TO TEACH HIM HOW TO:

1. Lift the lid and seat.
2. Take his pants and underwear down and stand close to the toilet.
3. Aim and pee, including teaching him how to direct the flow.
4. Adjust his stream, if needed, to keep the pee in the toilet.
5. Shake off any extra droplets of pee into the toilet.
6. Not step away until flow stops.
7. Take a small amount of toilet paper to wipe off the tip.
8. Pull up underwear and pants.
9. Clean up any misses.
10. Flush the toilet.

TIPS FOR PEEING STANDING UP

LIFT IT

One of the first things you will want to teach your son about peeing in the toilet standing up is to ALWAYS lift the toilet lid and seat. Then, when done, put the seat and lid back down.

HOLD ON

The natural tendency is for boys to try to hold their penis while peeing. Holding is more about directing the flow if needed.

If your son is lined up in front of the toilet and his penis is dangling over the toilet rim, his pee stream should go into the toilet effortlessly. Redirect if needed.

READY, AIM, FIRE

To help your son get the hang of aiming, you can create a bit of game out of it by throwing a couple Cheerios in the toilet that he can try to target and sink with his pee.

SHOW HIM HOW

Okay, dads–if you are comfortable with it, literally show him how it is done.

MAKE A MESS, CLEAN IT UP

At some point your son is going to miss and pee where you don't want him to. It is important that he learns to keep the pee in the toilet and if he misses, to clean it up after he is finished peeing.

PRACTICE, PRACTICE, PRACTICE

It's true that practice makes perfect. The more your son does it, the better he will become at aiming.

What the
flush now?

CHALLENGES & SOLUTIONS

Potty training can be stressful, especially when it doesn't go smoothly. We have outlined some of the more common challenges and provided tips and advice on how to handle them.

A LITTLE HELP PLEASE!

FINDING A BIT OF SUPPORT

Many parents today are busier than ever, and juggling the pressures of modern life and potty training can push parents to their wits' end. Sometimes parents need a little help getting through it.

THINGS TO KNOW

YOU ARE NOT ALONE

As frustrating and overwhelming as potty training can be, keep in mind that basically all kids learn to use the toilet. Every parent will need to navigate the ups and downs of potty training, so you are not alone.

EVERY CHILD IS DIFFERENT

Every child is unique and progresses at their own pace. What works for one child may not work for another. Although there are some typical timelines and approaches for potty training, you will need to adjust whatever method and technique you use to your child's specific needs.

GETTING HELP

Potty training can be far more challenging than you might have thought, and you might need to get the guidance of an expert. If that is the case, don't hesitate to ask for help.

WHO CAN HELP?

YOUR DOCTOR

Your child's primary health care provider is a great place to start. As your child's doctor, they will be the most familiar with your child's needs, and they can determine if there are any medical conditions that might be creating an issue.

TAP YOUR VILLAGE

Speaking to your friends and family can be a good source of practical advice.

EDUCATORS

If your child is in day care, the educators have a tremendous amount of experience and are an awesome source of know-how. They have more than likely worked with children with a wide variety of needs.

NANNIES

If you are working with a nanny, they might be able help provide some help.

POTTY TRAINING CONSULTANTS

There is a wide variety of consultants, ranging from groups to personal one-on-one consultations that provide guidance tailored to your specific needs.

- In-Home Consultants
- In-Person Training Classes
- Phone or Video Consultations
- Conferences and Seminars

ONLINE FORUMS

Sometimes, as parents, we just need a bit of reassurance and encouragement. Online forums or chats can provide that, but be sure to vet the information with your child's doctor to make sure it is right for you and your child.

VIDEOS & BOOKS

Check out online videos and books for information and solutions, but vet everything with your pediatrician to ensure that it is right for your child.

NOOOOOOO!
REFUSING TO USE THE POTTY

Yes, it's a common occurrence, and, yes, potty training can have its ups and downs.

HEY, WHAT GIVES?

Okay, what am I going to do now that my child will not even sit on the potty? Your toddler may just tell you **NO** outright or break down and begin crying or get angry at you.

Stay calm—this is not uncommon—don't force it.
The first thing is to double-check: Is your child truly ready for potty training? If your child is showing many of the signs of being ready but still refuses to use the potty, ask yourself what could be causing it.

WHAT IS IT?

POTTY TRAINING RESISTANCE

This occurs when a child appears to be ready for and capable of training but doesn't want to. Resistance may take several forms:

- Refusing to sit on the potty
- Holding their pee
- Continuing to pee or poop in a diaper
- Holding their poop

WHAT IS CAUSING IT?

There are several potential reasons for your child's refusal to use the potty.

THEY ARE AFRAID

Bathrooms and toilets can be scary for little ones. Several things could be creating that fear.

IT'S STINKY

Some children become so turned off by the smell of going to the potty that they actually refuse to go.

EMOTIONAL AND DEVELOPMENTAL READINESS

Every child develops at their own pace. Some children may not be ready as early as others and need more time. Patience and flexibility are key.

EXTERNAL STRESSES

Changes in the child's environment or routine can cause stress, which can negatively impact training. This can be caused by the arrival of a new baby, moving to a new home, starting a new school, or a divorce.

DISTRACTIONS

Your child may be too engaged in play. Getting your child to walk away from a fun activity can be really difficult and can be a very common issue during potty training.

MEDICAL ISSUES

There are several potential medical issues that can negatively impact potty training. Conditions like constipation, urinary tract infections, visual impairments, hearing loss, cerebral palsy, etc. Developmental disabilities like autism spectrum disorder and attention deficit/ hyperactivity disorder (ADHD) can also create challenges when training.

ASSERTING INDEPENDENCE

Your child might be trying to express their desire for more control, and not going to the potty is one of the those areas over which a toddler can exert control.

WANTING ATTENTION

At this age, your child might not be able to express themselves, as their verbal skills are still developing. By refusing to go, a child might be trying to get your attention in an attempt to communicate that they are anxious, fearful, or stressed.

I NO WANT!
HOW TO DEAL WITH NO

Your child refusing to potty train can be very upsetting. Here are some tips to help you deal with it.

QUICK TIP

If your child is 3 1/2 to 4 years old and still hasn't mastered or will not try using the potty, or if your child complains about pain or a burning sensation while peeing or pooping, you should discuss it with your pediatrician.

TIPS FOR DEALING WITH REFUSING TO GO

EASE THEIR FEARS

If your child is afraid of the flushing sound, wait to flush until after they leave the room. If they are afraid of falling into the toilet, support them while they go by holding their arms or legs.

MAKE NO NEGATIVE COMMENTS

Don't make negative comments about wearing diapers. Don't call your child a baby or make other disparaging remarks. Shaming them is not the answer.

READ ABOUT IT

Reading your child storybooks about using the potty can help ease a child's anxiety.

NOTE:

The American Academy of Pediatricians recommends starting potty training around 20 to 30 months. If your child is over three years old and you experience pushback, don't give in too easily. Try pressing on unless they have other concerns. Keep in mind, the older a child gets, the more difficult it can become.

REVIEW YOUR CHILD'S READINESS

Check if your child is truly ready for potty training. If your child is not ready, pause and try again after a couple of months. Never force, threaten, or punish them for not using the potty. It can lead to some negative results.

POO WITH YOU

You may have done it when you started potty training, but letting your child see you using the toilet can help them understand what to do and reduce the fear they may have.

BUYING A POTTY CHAIR

Consider buying a child-size potty chair instead of using the big toilet.

PRACTICE MORE

Encourage your child to try out the potty chair by sitting on it. Again, try to make it fun. Let them bring one of their favorite toys with them, or read them a story while they are sitting on the potty.

CREATE A ROUTINE

Bring your child to the potty on a regular schedule—for example, after every meal, first thing in the morning, before going to bed, before and after naps.

PRAISE, PRAISE, PRAISE

In the case of a child that refuses to go, be sure to praise them for every attempt to use the potty, even if they don't pee or poop.

ALWAYS BE POSITIVE

Children are like sponges—they absorb everything you do and say. They look to you for approval and encouragement, so always be positive and enthusiastic about all their efforts.

REWARDS

Some children respond well to rewards, so create a rewards chart to show their successes, and giving them a little something special when they get it right often works. Things like stickers or a treat can be effective.

TRY AGAIN LATER

When your child refuses to go, you can tell them it's okay, but add, "Let's try again in five minutes."

TANTRUM TIME
SCREAMING, CRYING, KICKING, OH MY!

Yes, meltdowns can happen during potty training too. Here is why and what to do.

WHAT IS IT?

TANTRUMS: Unfortunately, oh so familiar—an uncontrollable outburst of anger and frustration a young child has when they don't get their way.

WHY?

Tantrums can happen during potty training for several reasons, but they commonly occur when a child wants their diaper or pull-up back.

A tantrum can happen when you prompt your child to go to the potty. Your child might immediately throw themselves down on the floor and begin crying uncontrollably and screaming (a joy for every parent).

Potty training is a big deal to a child—it's something completely new, totally unfamiliar, and can cause them stress. No one likes change and a toddler, well, they hate it. They would prefer to have things stay just the way they were.

Many times, tantrums occur because the child wants to get your attention. Tantrums, in many cases, are part show for whomever is watching.

WHAT TO DO?

How we, as parents, respond to the tantrum is very important. There are several ways to address this depending on the child and the situation. When your child throws a tantrum, one of the first things you should do is make sure they are safe.

QUICK TIP

It has happened—your child is having a tantrum—how are you going to make it STOP?
One technique that can help calm a tantrum is distraction.
Try reading a book together, or introduce a toy, an activity, or something funny.

TIPS FOR DEALING WITH TANTRUMS

STAY CALM

This can be tough, but you really want to remain calm, patient, and in control.

FOLLOW THROUGH

Don't give in to the tantrum. You still want to follow through with going to the potty. So, tell your toddler they are going to go to the potty while you help them up and guide them to the bathroom. You don't want your child to learn that a tantrum gets them out of going to the potty. Be gentle and consistent about your expectations.

BE UNDERSTANDING

Your child is learning to control their emotions and to avoid acting impulsively. Don't ignore them. Instead, acknowledge your child's feelings. Ask them if they are scared, angry, etc., and then figure out what you can do to address their feelings.

CONSIDER A PAUSE

If your child is repeatedly having tantrums about potty training, it may be that they are not ready for it. It may be time to back off and try to reintroduce the potty training again later. This could be in a few weeks or months. You will need to assess the time needed for your child to be ready to try again.

POSITIVE REINFORCEMENT

Lean into giving positive reinforcement when your child exhibits good behavior. You may need to change the reward that you are currently using to something else that your child wants.

I NEED MY DIAPER

HOW TO DEAL WITH NOT POOPING IN POTTY

Your child is refusing to poop on the potty and will only poop in their diaper. Here is a technique that may help solve the problem.

WHAT TO DO?

While for many children potty training is a fairly straightforward process, for others, giving up the diaper can be a bit more complicated. Children have been in diapers for a long time, and wearing them can make them feel safe.

Helping your child to feel safe and move beyond using a diaper is about giving them control and allowing them to learn at their own pace. One way to address this is to transition gradually.

Part of the answer is to slow things down, gradually working on making progress. It may take several months.

TIPS FOR DITCHING THE DIAPER

Every child is different and is motivated by different things. Here are some techniques that have helped other parents and might help you too.

CONSIDER A PAUSE

First and foremost you should assess whether your child is truly ready for potty training and if it might be of value to take a short pause on training.

TIME FOR A LITTLE DISTRACTION

Children can become stressed when they try to go poop on the potty. The stress can cause them to tighten their muscles, making pooping hard. In some cases, distracting the child can help them to relax those muscles, allowing the poop to be let go. Try reading a book together or allowing your child to watch a video during their potty breaks.

PULL-UP AND TOILET

If your child tells you they want to poop in their diaper, tell them that they can wear it only if they stand next to or sit on the potty while pooping. Some parents have found success by progressively cutting bigger and bigger holes in the pull-up until they feel comfortable giving up the pull-up altogether. The key is to go very slowly and not cut too big of a hole in the pull-up.

REWARDS & TREATS

While we are not a fan of treats and toys as rewards for pooping in the potty, some children do respond to this type of reward. You will need to determine what is appropriate for your child.

ALL GONE

Some people have had success telling their child that this is the last pull-up. When they ask for another, tell them, "They're all gone."

NEVER FORCE IT.
SLOW DOWN.
SOME CHILDREN JUST NEED MORE TIME.

Mommy Hack

If your child says they are a baby and want their diaper back, you can say: *"You're not a baby anymore. I'm soooo proud of you for being such a BIG kid."*

FEAR OF THE TOILET

I AM NOT SURE ABOUT THIS THING

Fear of the toilet or toilet anxiety is very common and can take several forms. We have broken down why it occurs and what to do about it.

WHAT IS YOUR CHILD AFRAID OF?

FALLING INTO THE TOILET

Your little one is just that—little—and the hole in the seat of the toilet is much bigger than they are, so of course, they are afraid they might fall into the toilet.

FEAR OF LETTING IT GO

Some children see their poop and pee as a part of themselves and are afraid they are losing it if they let it go.

LOUD FLUSHING NOISE

The flushing sound, especially in loud public toilets, can create fear in some children.

GETTING SPLASHED

Some children have a fear of the water in the toilet and are afraid to get it on themselves.

IT'S COLD

Some children don't like to sit on a cold potty or toilet seat.

TIPS FOR REDUCING THE FEAR

PROVIDE SUPPORT

Securely hold your toddler so they realize there is no chance of them falling in. Tell them that you have them and you will not let them fall.

USE A SEAT REDUCER

Use a potty seat that inserts into the adult toilet seat. Your child will feel more secure because the hole is made to fit children.

FLUSHING TIPS

Check out the tips on the next page on how to deal with the fear of flushing.

PREVENT SPLASH

Try putting some toilet paper in the toilet to help prevent splashes. Also, wait to flush until your child is off the toilet.

TAKE IT SLOW

Start with no expectations and make sitting on the toilet something fun—read a book, sing songs. At first, don't even open the toilet lid—just let your child gradually get comfortable with sitting on the closed toilet.

WARM IT UP

Some children are bothered by the cold toilet seat. You can purchase a toilet seat warmer so that when your child sits down it's nice and toasty.

PLAY MUSIC

When your child goes to use the bathroom, play one of their favorite songs.

SHOW THEM

Have your child go with you to the bathroom when you need to use the toilet. Seeing you use the toilet and not being afraid may help alleviate some of their fear.

LET'S DECORATE

You and your child can decorate your home's toilet with fun stickers. This can give your child a better sense of ownership.

FEAR OF FLUSHING
IT'S TOO LOUD

You may relate to the scene of your toddler covering their ears and shaking their heads just before you flush the toilet. Fear of flushing is common among young children and can complicate potty training.

WHAT IS IT?

FEAR OF FLUSHING:

The fear and anxiety some children feel when flushing the toilet.

Children can be fearful of any and all types of toilets, but the ones that cause the most anxiety are:

- Public auto-flush toilets
- Airplane toilets

Mommy Hack
STICK IT TO IT

If your child is super scared of the flushing noise of the public auto-flush toilet, carry sticky notes with you, and when you use one of these toilets, stick the Post-it note over the sensor to keep it from flushing.

WHY?

LOUD SOUND

The very loud flushing noise, especially of some public toilets, can be very scary.

BEING FLUSHED AWAY

Some children are afraid that they or some part of them is going to be flushed down the toilet.

WHAT TO DO?

CREATE A DISTRACTION

One thing you can do is try and distract your child with something else.

CREATE A WELCOMING ENVIRONMENT

Have things in the bathroom that are fun and your child loves. They could be some toys or books—anything to make the space less scary.

FIGHT SOUND WITH SOUND

Use your cell phone to play some fun music your child likes.

CLOSE THE LID

Closing the toilet lid before you flush will help reduce the noise.

TALK

Reassure your child: "The toilet will not flush until we tell it to." To make sure it will not flush, try covering the sensor. Reinforce the idea that you will not let anything happen to them.

FLUSH AT THE END

Wait to flush the toilet until after your child is finished going, you have cleaned their bottom, and they are heading out of the bathroom or stall.

LET THEM FLUSH

Sometimes children feel more confident when they are in control.

TRY GRADUAL EXPOSURE

Allow your children to just observe the flushing without them peeing or pooping. Put some Cheerios in the toilet and let them have fun flushing them.

HEADPHONES

Use sound canceling headphones or earbuds to reduce or eliminate the sound.

FEAR OF PUBLIC TOILETS

WHAT ELSE CAN GO WRONG?

Oh, public toilets. We all know what a joy it is to use a public restroom, so it is not surprising that many children don't like them either.

WHY THE FEAR?

THEY ARE AN UNFAMILIAR PLACE

Public restrooms can be intimidating places because they are unfamiliar to your child.

THEY ARE LOUD

Public restrooms tend to be noisy places, from the banging stall doors to the noisy flushing toilets and the loud hand dryers.

THEY CAN BE SENSORY OVERLOAD

It could be there is just too much going on. The bright lights, the presence of strangers, the flushing and hand dryer noise all can be scary for kids.

THEY SMELL

Public restrooms can be awful-smelling places, which some kids hate—me too.

WHAT CAN YOU DO?

USE THE RESTROOM AT HOME

Before heading out, be sure to have your child use the bathroom at home.

BE A ROLE MODEL

Letting your child see you use the restroom can help them feel less scared.

GO SMALL

If possible, find public bathrooms that are small, one-person rooms that are more like the one at home. If possible, know ahead of time where the nicer bathrooms are.

BRING A TOILET INSERT

Bringing a toilet insert from home can help make sitting on an adult-size toilet less intimidating and reduce your child's fear of falling into the toilet.

HAND SANITIZER

Instead of using the sinks and dryers in the restroom, bring hand sanitizer and wet wipes to clean your child's hands after they go.

POST-IT NOTES

Cover the sensor with a sticky note so the toilet does not flush until you are ready for it to.

HEADPHONES

Bring some sound-canceling headphone or earmuffs along to reduce the noise of the flushing toilets and the hand dryers.

Mommy Hack

If your child can't stand the smell of public restrooms, consider carrying a small bottle of air freshener to spritz the bathroom or stall to help mask the yucky smell.

CONSTIPATION
WE ARE EXPERIENCING A BACKUP

If your child has experienced even one instance of painful pooping due to constipation, it can be enough to make them want to avoid pooping altogether.

WHAT IS IT?

CONSTIPATION:

A condition in which a person has difficulty pooping. The poop that is passed is usually small, hard, and dry. It can be uncomfortable or even painful. A person is generally considered to be constipated when bowel movements are fewer than three times a week or the poops are tiny pellets.

WHAT TO KNOW?

A child experiencing this condition may try not to go poop, trying instead to hold their poop to avoid the pain. This is a problem because the longer a child holds their poop, the harder and more difficult it will be to pass it.

SYMPTOMS

- Pain when pooping
- Hard and dry poop
- Straining when pooping
- Stomach pain
- Blood on the poop
- Poo-soiled underwear
- Typically fewer than three bowel movements a week

QUICK TIP

Having your child blow on a pinwheel or party favor while trying to poop can help relax their muscles. This can aid in helping them have a bowel movement. It is also important to make sure they have the right pottying posture (see page 51).

WHEN TO CALL THE DOCTOR

If your child has constipation or painful bowel movements, you should consult your pediatrician, especially if they have:

- Fever
- No desire to eat
- Abdominal swelling
- Weight loss
- Blood in poop
- Abdominal pain

TIPS FOR EASING CONSTIPATION

CHANGE DIET

Eating more fiber-rich foods like certain fruits and vegetables, beans, and whole grains can help move things along.

HYDRATE

Be sure your child is well hydrated by drinking plenty of fluids.

ENCOURAGE POTTYING

Make sure your child goes to the bathroom regularly. It can be helpful to create a toilet routine that sets specific times that your child goes to the potty to try and go.

REWARDS

Reward all your child's efforts to help encourage them to go. You could use stickers, treats, or some other small toys.

Mommy Hack

It is important to make sure your child's diet consists of fiber and quality fats and that they are well hydrated, so that when you begin potty training the poos are not too hard, as that can negatively affect training.

MEDICATION

Check with your health care provider to see if any medication that your child is taking could be causing the constipation.

GET MOVING

Make sure your child gets plenty of exercise and is active.

ACCIDENT, NOT AGAIN!

WHAT SEEMS TO BE THE PROBLEM?

Frequent accidents might signal something more is going on.

WHY DOES IT HAPPEN?

While accidents are a normal part of learning to use the potty and should be expected, there are some causes that require you to consult your pediatrician.

PHYSICAL ISSUES

PHYSICAL PROBLEMS

Accidents could be the result of:

- Constipation
- Urinary tract/kidney infection
- Small bladder
- Diabetes
- Urinary tract abnormalities
- Spina bifida
- Spinal cord injuries

OVERACTIVE BLADDER

Accidents can be the result of (OAB) Overactive Bladder. This is a condition that causes the muscles of the urinary tract to squeeze at the wrong time.

GENETICS

If you had physical issues that caused accidents when you were a child, it is possible your child might have them too.

EMOTIONAL ISSUES

STRESS

A child who is experiencing stress at school or home tends to have more accidents.

BULLYING

Being scared to use the school restroom because the child is afraid of being picked on.

BEHAVIORAL ISSUES

Some children may temporarily regress in their toilet training due to factors like attention-seeking behavior, sibling rivalry, or a desire to exert control, etc.

A CHANGE OF ROUTINE

Sometimes accidents can be caused by a change in the child's routine. That can range from being in an unfamilar place or your child experiencing an interruption in their daily routine. Events like a new sibling, changing homes, traveling, or starting a new school can contribute to accidents.

FEAR OF THE TOILET

This fear is especially common when using unfamilar toilets that can be noisy and scary.

DEVELOPMENTAL ISSUES

ATTENTION DEFICIT HYPERACTIVITY DISORDER (ADHD)

Children with ADHD have been found to become so preoccupied with an activity that they forget to go or don't completely go.

AUTISM SPECTRUM DISORDER (ASD)

It is common for children with autism to have accidents. Children with ASD may not be ready to be potty-trained, needing more time.

WHEN TO TALK TO YOUR DOCTOR

Always speak to your doctor if:

- There is blood in the pee or poop.
- Constipation is not resolved by diet, water, or exercise.
- You have questions or concerns about accidents.

UTI
URINARY TRACT INFECTION

A common infection that can occur in children and adults.

WHAT IS IT?

URINARY TRACT INFECTION (UTI):

Urinary tract infections are infections of the urinary system, which includes kidneys, ureters, bladder, and urethra. Most infections happen in the lower urinary tract—the bladder and the urethra.

Urinary tract infections tend to happen more often in girls than boys.

SYMPTOMS

Bladder and Urethra:

- Strong urge to pee
- Burning feeling when peeing
- Pee is cloudy
- Pee may have blood in it
- Pee has a bad smell
- Pelvic discomfort
- Tiredness

Kidney:

- Nausea
- Vomiting
- Fever
- Chills
- Back and side pain

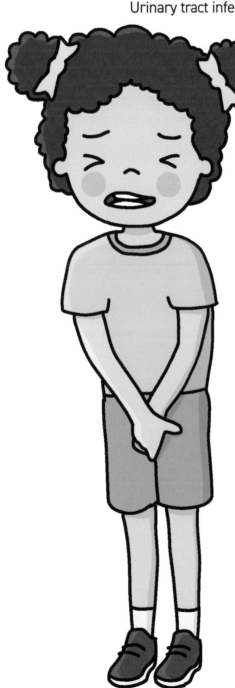

CAUSES

UTIs occur when bacteria cause an infection in the urinary tract. These bacteria can come from:

- Wiping the butt improperly after pooping.
- Sitting in a dirty diaper.
- Constipation.
- Holding pee even though the child has to go.
- Urine leaking back up into the ureters and kidneys.

PREVENTION

There is no way to entirely prevent UTIs, however, there are some things you can do to minimize the risk of your child getting one.

- Teach girls to wipe their bottoms from front to back with clean paper.
- Be sure your child drinks lots of fluids.
- Use loose cotton underwear rather than synthetic fabric underwear.
- Teach your child to fully empty their bladder.
- Peeing routinely throughout the day.
- Pooping daily or at least every other day.

TREATMENT

- Taking antibiotics
- Using a heating pad or medication to ease the pain
- Drinking plenty of water

NOTE: Although not causing UTIs, genital irritations can be the result of using bubble baths and fragranced laundry detergents and soaps.

CONTACT YOUR DOCTOR

Be sure to consult your pediatrician if you think your child might have a UTI and if the symptoms don't get better or worsen after treatment begins.

BAD-SMELLING PEE

OOH, STINKY!

Bad-smelling pee has several causes. When should you be concerned that it might indicate a health issue?

OVERVIEW

The smell of your child's urine will change over time and can be the result of several factors.

REASONS FOR THE SMELL?

Urine can have an odd or bad smell due to:

LIFESTYLE REASONS

- Eating certain foods
- Dehydration
- Certain medications
- Vitamin supplements

MEDICAL REASONS

- Illness
- Diabetes
- Imbalanced pH
- Certain metabolic disorders
- Urinary tract infections
- Certain genetic disorders
- Yeast infections

CONSULT YOU DOCTOR

If your child's urine has a bad smell, you should always consult your pediatrician to ensure that it is nothing serious. If the bad smell is accompanied by a fever, it can indicate something more serious, and you should speak with your doctor.

RED OR PINK URINE

BLOOD IN THE PEE

Discolored urine can be a sign of a health problem and can stress out any parent.

WHAT IS IT?

HEMATURIA: Blood that has leaked into your child's urine. There are two types:

Microscopic Hematuria: Blood in the urine that CANNOT be seen without a microscope.

Gross Hematuria: Blood in the urine that is visible to the eye, as the pee has turned red or pink.

WHERE DOES IT COME FROM?

Blood can get into the urine via the:

- Kidneys, which remove waste and water from the blood to make the urine.
- Ureters, which carry urine from the kidneys to the bladder.
- Bladder, which stores the urine.
- Urethra, through which the urine travels to leave the body.

WHAT CAUSES IT?

Children can get blood in their urine from:

- A bladder or kidney infection.
- A reaction to a medication.
- Injury to the kidneys or urinary tract.
- A genetic condition.
- Kidney stones.
- Kidney or bladder cancer.
- Extensive exercise.
- High calcium levels in the urine.

WHAT IS THE TREATMENT?

Depending on the cause of the hematuria, your child's doctor will determine the course of treatment.

PAUSE — DON'T PANIC

Discolored urine is scary and unnerving for all parents, but before you imagine the worst, first determine if your child might have eaten or drunk anything that could have caused the discoloration. Did they eat beets, cranberries, tomatoes, or something made with red food coloring—as these can cause pee and poo to have a red color.

Regardless, you should always contact your child's doctor to confirm the cause and appropriate treatment, if any.

REGRESSION
NOT SO FAST; WE'RE NOT DONE YET!

It can be frustrating when you felt your child was making progress or had achieved the milestone of potty training only to have to start over. Here is what you need to know about handling regression.

WHAT IS IT?

POTTY TRAINING REGRESSION:

When a child who has been or is in the process of potty training begins reverting back to their previous behavior.

This may take the form of suddenly starting to have regular accidents or they want to wear their diapers again. Regression is not a couple accidents every now and again—it's when the child is consistently and regularly having accidents or demanding diapers.

Your child may express regression in several ways:

- Having several accidents a day.

- No longer peeing in the potty.

- No longer pooping in the potty.

- Asking to wear diapers again.

- No longer self-initiating going to the potty.

COMMON CAUSES OF REGRESSION

PREGNANCY OR BIRTH OF A SIBLING

Mom is pregnant with a new baby or a new sibling has joined the family.

CHANGE IN ROUTINE

There is a change of routine, such as attending a new school/day care, or the arrival of a new caregiver or a change in caregivers.

NEW HOME

Your family is in the process of moving or has moved into a new home.

ILLNESS OF CHILD OR FAMILY MEMBER

The child or a family member is very sick or has a medical problem.

URINARY TRACT INFECTION

Child may have a urinary tract infection.

TRAUMA

Child may have experienced a trauma.

CONSTIPATION

Your child may have constipation. This can cause painful bowel movements, which your child might be trying to avoid by not going.

DEATH IN THE FAMILY

Someone in the family has died.

FAMILY CONFLICT

The child may be stressed as a result of family problems, for example, marital conflict or divorce.

REGRESSION
HOW TO FIX IT?

Regression can be caused by many factors, many of which can be addressed. Here is what you need to know.

TIPS FOR HANDLING REGRESSION

DON'T PUNISH

Regression can be very frustrating, but don't get angry or punish your child, as it can make the situation even worse.

IDENTIFY THE SOURCE

Work on understanding what may be causing the regression. Determine if it is truly a regression or just random accidents. Are there any patterns to the accidents, or has there been any stressful event that may have triggered the accidents?

LET'S TALK

If you think a stress-related event might have caused the regression, in a calm and positive tone of voice, talk with your child. Try to understand the underlying issue so you can help them cope with it or ease their fears.

CREATE A SCHEDULE

Be sure to set specific times for your child to go to the potty, and consistently follow it. A schedule might be when they get up, before and after meals, and at nap and bedtime. Or it could be as simple as every couple of hours.

KEEP YOUR COOL

Remain calm and encouraging even if there are accidents. Your child will pick up on your stress or frustration, which can have negative consequences.

TALK WITH YOUR DOCTOR

Consult your pediatrician or other health care provider to get their guidance and help, especially if a medical issue is the cause of the regression.

RESTART THE PROCESS

It may be necessary to start the process over again. You will want to be super positive and encouraging, just like you were the first time.

TRAINING: ROUND 2

When you start over, keep in mind those things that worked and those that were less successful. Adjust your approach to reinforce those aspects that worked for your child, and drop those that did not.

CLARIFY EXPECTATIONS

Be sure to make it clear that you are beginning again and that your toddler will need to resume going on the potty.

MOVE THE POTTY

If your child is having a hard time getting to the potty in time, consider moving it closer to where your child is.

TRAINING PANTS

If nothing seems to work, consider going to training pants instead of going back to diapers.

POSITIVE REINFORCEMENT

Be a strong supporter of your child's efforts, and give them as much encouragement as possible.

DEAL WITH THE FEAR

If your child is scared of the sound of the toilet flushing, hold off on the flushing until after they are done and gone.

CHILDREN WITH DISABILITIES

A FEW HELPFUL THOUGHTS

Potty training can be challenging for any parent. It can be even more complicated with children who have disabilities.

While this book can help most parents potty train their little one, it may not be ideal for everyone, especially for those training toddlers with disabilities. They may require additional support and modified training methods.

WHAT IS IT?

Children With Disabilities:

Refers to individuals who have a condition or combination of conditions that make learning or other activities difficult or who require assistance when doing them.

TYPES OF DISABILITIES

Physical Disabilities:

- Cerebral palsy
- Spinal cord injury
- Spina bifida
- Genetic syndromes

Developmental/Behavioral Disabilities:

- Autism
- ADHD
- Oppositional behavior
- Sensory processing disorder

Physical Impairment:

- Blindness
- Deafness

TIPS FOR TRAINING KIDS WITH DISABILITIES

STAY CALM

Try to remain calm and patient when accidents happen. Your child will pick up on your emotions, so staying composed can help reduce their anxiety and yours.

ENGAGE THE TEAM

When potty training a child with disabilities, it is best to engage the full support of your team, your family, nanny, caregivers, teachers, and day care. Get everyone on board with the strategies and tactics you will be applying. You should also make sure everyone has all the supplies necessary.

SUPPORT GROUPS

Training special needs children can be stressful and overwhelming at times. Joining a group for parents with children who have disabilities can be very helpful.

BE PATIENT

It's important to understand that the process of potty training will more than likely take longer--in some cases, much longer.

COMMUNICATION ISSUES

If your child has difficulty communicating, consider using simple pictures or visuals to help get the idea across. Ideally, you should use verbal communication along with the pictures.

Pull down pants   Sit on toilet   Wipe   Pull up pants   Wash hands   Dry hands

GET PROFESSIONAL HELP

If you are struggling despite your best efforts, you may need to speak with an expert on your child's particular disability.

NOTE: If you are going to be training a child with a disability, you should consult your pediatrician for recommendations and whether they feel you should engage additional experts.

A dry
night's
sleep

OVERNIGHT TRAINING

What you need to know about the difference between daytime and overnight training, tips, and advice.

OVERNIGHT TRAINING

POTTY TRAINING IS NOT OVERNIGHT TRAINING

Reaching the milestone of staying dry all through the night is another developmental milestone and is not the same as daytime potty training. Here are a few things you ought to know.

DAYTIME TRAINING VS. OVERNIGHT TRAINING

Daytime potty training is **NOT** the same as overnight potty training.

QUICK TIP

In order to successfully overnight train your child, they must have transitioned from the crib to a big-kid bed and have unobstructed access to the bathroom.

OVERNIGHT TRAINING

Successful nighttime potty training means that a sleeping child recognizes the need to go to the bathroom and either holds it until morning or wakes up and successfully goes to the bathroom.

WHAT TO KNOW

Even if your child has mastered going diaper free during the day, they may still have difficulty holding it all night. Most toddlers are not ready for overnight training just because they are daytime trained. Overnight training may take a bit longer.

Being able to remain dry overnight means that both your child's bladder and their brain have matured enough that they hold their pee and wake up when they feel the need to go.

DON'T STRESS!

Your child can be potty-trained during the day and still wear a pull-up at night for a while longer—it is OK. However, if your child is showing signs of holding it throughout the night, ditch the pull-up.

WHAT TO KNOW

Every child is different and develops at their own pace, but most should be able to stay dry or use the bathroom at night between the ages of five and six years old.

5 to 6 Years Old

AVERAGE AGE A CHILD SHOULD BE ABLE TO
STAY DRY ALL NIGHT

BED-WETTING
WHAT IS NORMAL AND WHAT IS NOT?

A child may use the toilet well during the day long before they are dry throughout the night. Depending on the child, it may take several more months or even years before your child is able to stay dry all night.

WHAT TO KNOW?

Most children outgrow bed-wetting on their own, but some need a little help. In some cases, bed-wetting may be a sign of an underlying condition.

WHEN DOES IT STOP?

Most children outgrow bed-wetting between the ages of five and six.

CAUSES

Several factors can cause bed-wetting:

- Family history of bed-wetting
- Emotional stress
- Deep sleeper
- Small bladder
- Constipation
- Stress or fear

- Slow physical development
- Delayed bladder development
- Diabetes
- Urinary tract infection
- Vaginitis

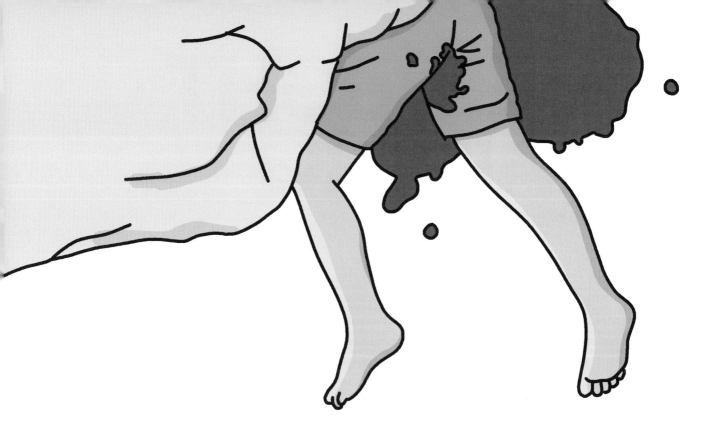

WHAT TO DO?

Start logging your child's toileting and wetting routine.

WHEN TO SPEAK TO YOUR DOCTOR

- If your child is still wetting the bed after seven years old.

- If your child stayed dry throughout the night, and then starts wetting the bed again.

- Your child has pain when peeing, or urine is pink or red.

Before you meet with your pediatrician or health care provider, start noting when your child goes to the toilet, has accidents, and/or wets the bed.

What to note:

- Number of times your child goes pee
- Number of times your child goes poop
- Type and amount of drinks
- Number of daytime accidents
- Number of nighttime accidents

OVERNIGHT TRAINING
A FEW HELPFUL TIPS

TIPS FOR OVERNIGHT TRAINING

LIMIT LIQUIDS
One to two hours before bedtime, cut out all fluids.

USE THE POTTY
Have your child go to the bathroom one hour before and again immediately before bedtime.

GO AGAIN
When you go to bed, you might want to wake your child and have them try to go to the bathroom.

REMIND THEM
Tell your child what to do if they wake up during the night and need to go.

NIGHTLIGHTS
Be sure that there is enough light in their room and the bathroom so that they can see. You might even help them pick the nightlight with their favorite character.

MATTRESS COVER
Use a mattress cover to prevent damaging the mattress and make cleanup easier.

USE AN ALARM

You can try setting an alarm to wake you so that you can take your child to the potty in the middle of night. This should only be a short-term thing. You don't want your child to become dependent on you waking them up. Consider using a bed-wetting alarm for your child.

DAYTIME TRAINING FIRST

Once your child has successfully completed the daytime potty training and has been using the potty on a regular basis, start beginning overnight dryness training.

REDUCE STRESS

Make the bedtime ritual relaxing to help your child wind down. Stress in children can hinder progress and cause setbacks.

TRAINING PANTS/PULL-UPS

Switching to training pants or pull-ups helps to make it easier for your children to pull them up and down by themselves.

REASSURANCE & PRAISE

Accidents are going to happen! No scolding, blaming, or punishment for accidents. Instead, stay positive and praise any and all successes.

ASKING FOR HELP

Let your child know that they can wake you up to help them go to the bathroom at night.

QUICK TIP

Just like daytime potty training, the time it takes for nighttime potty training varies from child to child.

It depends on the child's physical development.

Let's talk
shit about
potty training.

TRAINING SCRIPTS

Practical tips, phrases, and ways to speak with your child to help them achieve potty training success and reduce the overall stress for both of you.

SAY WHAT?
HELPFUL SCRIPTS

We have compiled talking points to help you navigate some of the various situations that may arise. Always use an upbeat and positive tone of voice when speaking to your child.

BEFORE YOU MOVE TO UNDERWEAR

While your child is still in pull-ups, begin to insert the idea—without being negative—that being wet or in a dirty diaper is not good and feels yucky.

"Your diaper is dirty. Let's put on a clean one."

"Your diaper is wet. Let's get you into a clean one."

WHEN YOU GO TO THE BATHROOM

When taking your child to the bathroom with you to see you going, here are some things you could say to encourage them to imitate your behavior.

"I feel the need to pee, so I'm going to the potty."

"I had a lot to drink, and now my body is telling me I need to go potty. Do you want to come with me?"

"Do you hear that sound? I am peeing in the toilet."

"You want to help me say goodbye to the (pee or poo) by flushing the toilet? Bye (pee or poo)."

"Soon you will be able to wear big (boy or girl) underwear and go potty just like Mommy and Daddy."

"I feel I have to go pee or potty. Want to come with me?"

WHEN AN ACCIDENT OCCURS

When accidents happen, stay positive and have your child help clean it up.
You can say things like:

"Thanks for letting me know you had an accident. Let's clean it up and try again later."

"Oh no, pee goes in the potty, not on the floor."

"I see you are wet. Let's go get some dry clothes."

"Oops, you peed on the floor. Let's try to get it in the potty next time."

"You pooped/peed in your pants. Poop goes in the potty. Next time you feel the poop coming, let's go sit on the potty."

"We did not make it to the potty in time. Next time you feel you need to pee, let's go to the potty and get the pee in the potty."

" (Child's name), you were supposed to tell me when you need to go to the potty. Now your underwear and pants are wet (or dirty). You need to let me know when you have to go. Let's get you changed and clean up the accident."

QUICK TIP

When your child has an accident, you want to avoid saying, "It's okay." You don't want your child to think it was okay to pee or poop in their pants.

SCRIPTS
HOW BEST TO TALK WITH YOUR CHILD
Always use an upbeat and positive tone of voice when speaking to your child.

WIPING & WASHING CORRECTLY

Here is what you might say when your child wipes and washes their hands correctly:

"Great job wiping today."

"You washed your hands really well."

SUCCESSFULLY PEEING OR POOPING

Here is what you might say:

*"You did it. You (peed/pooped) in the potty.
You felt the need to (pee or poo), and you listened to your body
and let it go."*

*"Wow, you (peed or pooped) in the potty. You did
a great job—you must feel better letting all that go.
How do you feel?"*

*"Wow, you felt the need to (pee or poop) and went to the
potty to (pee or poop), I am so proud of you!"*

BEFORE LEAVING THE HOUSE:

Here are a few things you could say when you are going out to run ERRANDS.

"Before we go to _____ let's try and use the potty."

WHEN YOU GET A LITTLE PUSHBACK

Here is what you might say when you receive a little pushback.

"Thank you for sitting on the potty and trying to go."

"Let's go to the potty and then you can come back and _____."

"Let's go to the potty. The sooner we go, the sooner you can get back to _____."

"Please don't tell me no. (Peeing or pooping) in your underwear is not what we do. (Pee or poop) always goes in the potty."

"Thank you for sitting on the potty. We can try again in a little bit."

Wanting their diaper:

"You're not a baby anymore. I am soooo proud of you for being such a BIG kid."

WHEN THEY SHOW SIGNS OF NEEDING TO GO:

*"It looks like you need to use the potty.
Let's go sit on the potty."*

"(Child's name), you are (whatever sign). Your body is telling you it needs to go to the potty. Let's go to the toilet."

*"Good morning! First, we'll sit on the potty,
and then we'll have breakfast."*

SCRIPTS
HOW BEST TO TALK WITH YOUR CHILD

Always use an upbeat and positive tone of voice when speaking to your child.

ASKING TO GO POTTY

Instead of asking if they need to go potty, which they are more than likely going to say NO to, you can say:

"Time to go potty."   or,   *"It's time for a potty break."*

Children at this age are beginning to want a sense of control and have a growing desire for independence. If your child has this inclination, you might ask with a choice:

"Would you like to go to the potty in two minutes or five minutes?"

"We have to be sure to listen to our bodies. When your body tells you it needs to go, we go to the potty."

"When you have the feeling of needing to go pee or poop, let me know, and we can go to the potty to pee or poop."

USE NATURAL TRANSITIONS

There are points throughout the day that lend themselves to going to the potty, like before or after meals, naps, or bed.

"We are getting ready for lunch. Let's try and go potty before we eat."

"We're about to eat dinner. Let's go potty before we eat."

AFTER REMAINING DRY

Things are going well—what to say to be encouraging:

"I love how you are such a big boy today, and you are learning to go pee on the potty."

"That's a whole day with no potty accidents! You have definitely earned a high five."

CAUGHT MID-PEE/POOP

You may catch your child mid-pee and poop many times. Here is what you can say:

"Oh, you're peeing/pooping. Let's go to the potty and get the rest of it in the potty."

"Oh, you're peeing/pooping—try and hold it— let's get the rest in the potty."

" When you feel the poop starting to come, let's run to the potty to sit and let it out in the potty."

WHAT <u>NOT</u> TO ASK

Don't ask if they need to go to the potty, as most kids will immediately say NO. Instead, say:

"Let's go to the potty and try and go."

"Tell me when you need to go potty."

WHAT <u>NOT</u> TO SAY

"You're being bad."

"That is really bad."

"Why did you pee on the floor?"

SCRIPTS
HOW BEST TO TALK WITH YOUR CHILD

DRY UNDERWEAR

Some parents go straight to character underwear when training. Others put their child's favorite character underwear on their child with a pull-up over that to minimize messes. Both methods will help teach the child to recognize that they had an accident.

In addition, some children don't like the feeling of being wet, so wearing underwear prompts them to try not to pee. You can reinforce this by saying:

"Be sure to keep your (<u>character's name</u>) dry. They don't like to be wet."

*"Make sure you don't pee on (<u>character's name</u>).
Yucky—poor (<u>character's name</u>) will not like that."*

When you are checking to see if they are dry, say:

*"Is your underwear dry?
I'm so proud of you keeping your underwear (or
<u>character's name</u>) dry."*

WHEN YOU ARE OUT & ABOUT

Before you head out on a short trips:

"We are going to be going to _____. Let's sit on the potty and try to go before we leave."

"We can go outside once you have tried to _____."

"I am going to try and go potty before we leave to_____. Let's you and I try together."

When you are out and about:

"While we are out, if you feel you need to (pee or poop), tell me so we can make a bathroom stop, and you can go."

FINAL THOUGHTS
WORDS OF ADVICE

Potty training is stressful and it can be hard—so it's no surprise that we, as parents, worry, worry, worry. But you need to cut yourself some slack.

YOU CAN DO THIS!

Potty training at times can be discouraging, especially when it doesn't go as planned or it doesn't happen how and when "experts" say it's supposed to. Stop worrying. Every child is unique and develops at their own pace, so it's best not to compare yourself or your child to others.

We're here to tell you that it will all be okay. You are not alone in feeling stressed, frustrated, and sometimes even angry—yes angry. We all have these feelings at various points along our parenting journey, but potty training can really push one's buttons.

It is worth understanding that pottying is a developmental milestone that, in the end, all kids reach at some point. You can't force it. The best you can do is support and encourage your child throughout the process. Ultimately, it's up to them when they are ready. You know your child better than anyone, and no matter what method or technique you use, you will more than likely have to tailor it to fit your child and their unique needs.

Stop beating yourself up or feeling like you are a failure or a horrible parent. Be patient and loving not only to your child but to yourself. You can and will do this!

BIG THANKS
ACKNOWLEDGMENT

Many thanks to my patient and brilliant partners and contributors in the development of this book and the Simplest series, especially to Design Studio Press and my editors. Thank you to the countless educators and health care professionals who so generously shared their knowledge and expertise with me. Thanks to the countless number of parents who openly and honestly shared their experiences, both good and bad. Finally, a heartfelt thank you to my family, who were partners in all of this. They encouraged me, listened to me, and helped me through countless drafts. Thank you so much, and much love.

INDEX

A

B

naptime

    pull-ups and, 55

    schedule, 61, 145

    training, 71–72

overnight training, 151–56

    advice, 155–56

    bed-wetting, 153–54

    liquids and, 71, 155

    pull-ups and, 55

    readiness and, 151–52

parent

    books and videos for, 24, 118

    demonstrating toileting with, 24, 41–42, 84, 131

    readiness, 15–16

pause, when to, 16, 122, 124–26

pediatrician

    when to consult, 16, 106, 118, 121

        accidents, 135–36

        bed-wetting, 154

        constipation, 134

        discolored urine, 141–42

        for children with disabilities, 148

        regression, 146

        urine with bad smell, 140

        UTI, 138

personality

    impact on training, 11–12

    types of, 11–12

phrases to use

    prompts and reminders, 68–69

    to discuss pottying at day care with child, 108

    to illustrate bodily sensations, 31–32, 60

    to introduce potty chair, 35

    to praise success, 70, 88

    training, day 1, 63–64, 66–71

    training, day 2, 73–74

    when accidents occur, 66–68, 91

    when demonstrating, 41–42

    when encountering resistance, 126

    when preparing to train, 33–34, 63–64

    when selecting underwear, 47–48

    when teaching handwashing, 81–82

    when transitioning to underwear, 73–74

planning

    home, 49–50, 95

    meals, 96

potty breaks

    before travel, 79, 105

    consistency and, 73

    liquids and, 65

    routine, 73, 80

    when to take, 61, 65, 76

potty chair. See training chairs

pottying steps, 70

Welcome to
The Simplest Baby community, share with friends and family our must-have titles!

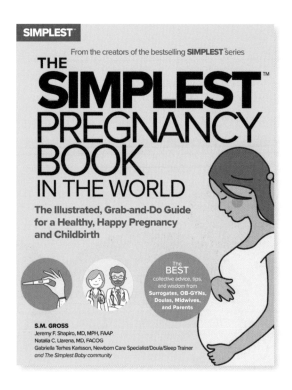

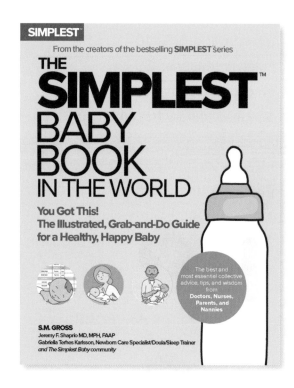

The best parent resources to simplify pregnancy, childbirth, and the first year!

Having a baby can be complex and stressful. *The Simplest* series makes pregnancy, childbirth, and bringing up baby easier, while helping to reduce the stress and creating the confidence for a healthy, happy pregnancy and baby, so you can spend more time enjoying what is one of the most magical experiences of your life.

Scan this QR codes for quick access to *The Simplest Baby Book in the World.*
Get yours today!

The Illustrated, Grab-and-Do Guides for a Healthy, Happy Pregnancy, Childbirth, and Baby

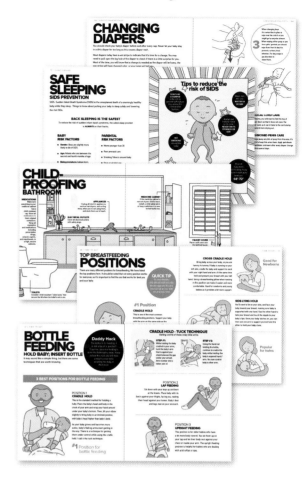

PREGNANCY BASICS MADE EASY • INSTANT KNOW-HOW • BABY BASICS MADE EASY

THE MUST-HAVE LISTS • THE BEST EXPERT ADVICE • BREASTFEEDING 101

GETTING BABY TO SLEEP • INTRODUCING SOLIDS • BABY SAFETY • PARENT TIPS

AND SOOOO MUCH MORE!

The BEST and most essential collective advice, tips, and wisdom from:
Doctors, Nurses, Surrogates, Doulas, Midwives, Nannies, and Parents

CONTRIBUTORS
THE TEAM

DR JEREMY SHAPIRO
MD, MPH, FAAP

Dr. Jeremy Shapiro has been practicing general pediatrics in Encino, California, over the past 20 years. He has shared this journey with his wife and three children, who have motivated him to be a better husband, father, pediatrician, and person. The joy of caring for a child from birth until adulthood is what initially inspired him to become a pediatrician, and he treasures each and every day he is able to continue doing so. Dr. Shapiro also appreciates the 10-year period he spent in local hospital leadership, culminating with the position of the chief of the medical staff during the height of the COVID-19 epidemic; an experience and time unlike any other. He is also very thankful for being able to participate in the Simplest Baby series, as it is one further way he is able to help parents on life's most special journey.

To learn more about Dr Shapiro, visit:

https://simplestbaby.com/expert-contributors/

SUZI SCHWARTZ
Newborn Care, Potty Training Expert,
New Parent Coach, and Sleep Trainer

Suzi Schwartz is the owner of OC Newborn Nanny in Orange County, California, and is a seasoned potty training expert. She started her career more than 25 years ago, working in day cares and preschools, and then transitioned to supporting families in their private homes. Suzi also supports countless families outside of California with customized virtual potty training support services.

Suzi is uniquely qualified as a certified potty training expert. In addition to her numerous certifications and ongoing education from other industry leaders, Suzi has successfully potty trained more than 1,000 children. She uses personalized, nonmedical, evidence-based strategies and best practices to address a wide variety of common challenges, such as fear of release, refusal, withholding, nap and night training, constipation, and encopresis. In addition to being a potty training expert, Suzi is also a certified professional newborn care specialist, new parent coach, pediatric sleep consultant and trainer, certified postpartum doula, and parent advocate.

Suzi married her husband in 1995, and together they have raised two boys. She contributes her career success in part to her own lived parenting experiences. She understands firsthand the highs and lows of raising children.

Learn more about Suzi:

Website: OCNewBornNanny.com

Potty Training Landing Page: OCNewBornNanny.com/pottytrain

Email: ocnewbornnanny@gmail.com

Facebook: Facebook.com/OCNewBornNanny

Instagram: Instagram.com/ocnewbornnanny